Living Faiths

Judaism

Sue Schraer

Series Editor: Janet Dyson   **Consultant:** Robert Bowie

OXFORD
UNIVERSITY PRESS

OXFORD
UNIVERSITY PRESS

Great Clarendon Street, Oxford, OX2 6DP, United Kingdom

Oxford University Press is a department of the University of Oxford. It furthers the University's objective of excellence in research, scholarship, and education by publishing worldwide. Oxford is a registered trade mark of Oxford University Press in the UK and in certain other countries

© Oxford University Press 2013

The moral rights of the authors have been asserted

First published in 2013

British Library Cataloguing in Publication Data
Data available

ISBN-13: 978-0-19-838898-2

13

Paper used in the production of this book is a natural, recyclable product made from wood grown in sustainable forests. The manufacturing process conforms to the environmental regulations of the country of origin.

Printed and bound by CPI Group (UK) Ltd, Croydon, CR0 4YY

Acknowledgements

The publishers would like to thank the following for permissions to use their photographs:

Acknowledgements

The publishers would like to thank the following for permissions to use their photographs:

Cover: Gareth Boden/OUP; **p11:** Ron Stilling/Associated Newspapers/ Rex Features; **p12:** Robert Harding Picture Library Ltd/Alamy; **p14:** Ocean/Corbis; **p16:** Alisdair Macdonald/Rex Features; **p17:** INTERFOTO/Alamy; **p20:** World Religions Photo Library/Alamy; **p24:** Israel images/Alamy; **p26:** Royal 2 A. XXII, f.14v/The British Library Board; **p26:** Eitan Simanor/Alamy; **p30:** diligent/Shutterstock; **p32t:** Getty Images; **p32b:** Getty Images; **p39:** Jeffrey Blackler/Alamy; **p40** clockwise from top right: imagebroker/Alamy; Howard Grill/ Shutterstock; World Religions Photo Library/Alamy; Ted Spiegel/ CORBIS; **p41:** AFP/Getty Images; **p43:** Hanan Isachar/Getty Images; **p45t:** Chameleons Eye/Rex Features; **p45b:** blueeyes/Shutterstock; **p47t:** Maksim Dubinsky/Shutterstock.com; **p47b:** Tim Klein/Galeries/ Corbis; **p53:** David Grossman/Alamy; **p55:** ZUMA Wire Service/ Alamy; **p56:** with kind permission from Elke Reva Sudin; **p57:** Sipa Press/Rex Features; **p59:** Keidar/Israel Sun/Rex Features; **p60t:** PUNIT PARANJPE/Reuters/Corbis; **p60b:** Getty Images; **p61:** Getty Images; **p63:** PhotoStock-Israel/Alamy; **p66:** Godong/Robert Harding World Imagery/Corbis; **p71l:** with kind permission from Nina Hollington; **p71r:** The Washington Post/Getty Images; **p72:** Jim West/Alamy; **p74:** Eddie Gerald/Alamy; **p75:** silver-john/Shutterstock; all other photos by OUP

Illustrations: Gareth Clarke

From the author, Sue Schraer: It has been a great privilege to write for this exciting Living Faiths Series – my grateful thanks to the OUP editorial team. Appreciation also goes to the following people who assisted both directly and indirectly: Lizzie McWhirter, from RE Today; Jillian Dunstan, Head Teacher of Mathilda Marks-Kennedy Jewish Primary School; Pam Goldsmith of the Reform Movement; Rabbi Pete Tobias of The Liberal Synagogue Elstree; Judi Newman; and most of all, Mike Schraer for his knowledge and constant support. I am indebted to the three families from across the Jewish religious spectrum who generously and articulately participated, and shared – with enthusiasm and sincerity – their experiences, beliefs, and different stances on living life as a Jew in Britain today.

I dedicate this book to the memory of Naomi Felder whose life was so tragically cut short.

OUP wishes to thank the Reznik, Morris and Walton families for agreeing to take part in the case study films and to be photographed for this title. We would also like to thank Simon Goulden, education consultant; Rabbi Pete Tobias of The Liberal Synagogue Elstree; and Ann Angel, MA, PGCE, Jewish education consultant, for reviewing this book.

We are grateful for permission to reprint extracts from the following copyright material:

Extracts from The Complete Artscroll Machzor (Mesorah Publications, 1987), reprinted by permission of the copyright holders, Artscroll/ Mesorah Publications, Ltd.

Extracts from the Tanakh: The Holy Scriptures (JPS, 1985), copyright © 1985, 1999 by the Jewish Publication Society, Philadelphia, reprinted by permission of the University of Nebraska Press.

Contents

Introduction

What's it like to be Jewish?

The *Living Faiths* series helps you to learn about religion by meeting some young people and their families in the UK. Through the case studies in this book you will find out first-hand how their faith affects the way they live and the moral and ethical decisions they make. The big question you will explore is: What does it *mean* to be Jewish in twenty-first century Britain?

The icons indicate where you can actually hear and see young people sharing aspects of their daily lives through film, audio and music. This will help you to reflect on your own experiences, whether you belong to a religion or have a secular view of the world.

Key to icons

Image gallery   Audio   Film   Worksheet   Interactive Activity

The Student Book features

Starter activities get you thinking as soon as your lesson starts!

Activities are colour coded to identify three ways of exploring the rich diversity found within and between faiths. Through the questions and activities you will learn to:

- **think like a theologian**: these questions focus on understanding the nature of religious belief, its symbolism and spiritual significance
- **think like a philosopher**: these questions focus on analysing and debating ideas
- **think like a social scientist**: these questions focus on exploring and analysing why people do what they do and how belief affects action

You will be encouraged to think creatively and critically; to empathize, evaluate and respond to the views of others; to give reasons for your opinions and make connections; and draw conclusions.

Useful Words define the key terms which appear in bold, to help you easily understand definitions. Meanings of words are also defined in the glossary.

Reflection

There will be time for you to reflect on what you've learned about the beliefs and practices of others and how they link to your own views.

Assessment

At the end of each chapter there is a final assessment task which helps you to show what you have learned.

Ways of helping you to assess your learning are part of every chapter:

- unit objectives set out what you will learn
- it's easy to see what standards you are aiming for using the 'I can' level statements
- you're encouraged to discuss and assess your own and each other's work
- you will feel confident in recognizing the next steps and how to improve.

We hope that you will enjoy reading and watching young people share their views, and that you will, in turn, gain the skills and knowledge to understand people with beliefs both similar to, and different from, your own.

Janet Dyson
(Series Editor)

Robert Bowie
(Series Consultant)

Meet the Families!

In this book, you will meet several young Jewish families from across the UK. You can read about their thoughts and views on various topics covered in the book, and also watch their full interviews on the *Judaism Kerboodle*.

The Reznik family

Laurie and Jordan live with their parents and younger brother, Adam, in North London. They are members of a Modern Orthodox synagogue and go to a local faith-based school. They enjoy spending Shabbat (the Sabbath) with family and friends. They also enjoy doing activities together like trampolining, swimming, top golf, or just sitting on the couch reading.

The Morris family also lives in London. The three sisters, Shuli, Nina and Shifra, are active members of a Reform synagogue with their parents. They like singing, walking, swimming, laughing and talking. Shuli likes Latin and Greek. Nina likes the Beatles and Shifra likes cake!

The Morris family

The Walton family

Hollie and Jack live with their parents in Hertfordshire, and they go to a local Liberal synagogue. Hollie likes to play guitar and teach in the synagogue's religion school, and Jack likes to play sports.

Overview

At around 3500 years old, Judaism is one of the world's most ancient faiths. Its tiny population (less than 1% of the world's total) has included many famous and influential people, such as Einstein, Freud and Marx – as well as many artists, politicians, writers, musicians, philosophers, entrepreneurs and scientists.

As traditional Judaism teaches that a Jew is the child of a Jewish mother, Jews are a distinct ethnic group (although it is possible to convert to Judaism). In addition to this ethnic identity, an observant Jew follows the laws given by God as set out in the most sacred Jewish text called the Torah, or Five Books of Moses. This includes a moral code for living (called the Ten Commandments), which is also at the root of Christianity.

Central to Judaism is the special relationship, or covenant, between God and Jews, His 'Chosen People'. Jews believe that God spoke to the world through them – revealing how to live righteous lives. As a 'light to the nations', God wanted the Jewish people to set an example. At the time, the Jews were nomads, and were promised a land in exchange for following these instructions.

There are a number of Movements within Judaism, which interpret the Jewish laws differently. The most Orthodox Jews strictly observe the rules from the Torah, as detailed in the Talmud, which govern every aspect of their daily lives. The Progressive Movement (including Reform and Liberal Judaism) has adapted laws in an attempt to modernize ancient practices.

The purpose of keeping laws is to bring an age of peace to the world, either, as traditional Judaism believes, through a single leader (the Messiah) or a human effort to repair the world (bringing about the Messianic Age).

Hebrew is the language used for prayer. Jews worship in a synagogue, although prayer may also take place at home or elsewhere. Throughout the year, sections of the Torah are read in Hebrew in synagogue from a hand-written scroll.

Keeping a special day of rest and prayer, Shabbat, is a key element in the practice of Judaism. It begins every Friday evening and ends at nightfall on Saturday, with the sighting of three stars. This recalls the creation of the universe, when God rested on the seventh day.

For many Jews, a key aspect of Jewish life is the practice of keeping kosher (the observance of Jewish dietary laws). Those animals that may not be eaten, such as pig and shellfish, are listed in the Torah.

Festivals occur during the year, and they often recall significant historical events or the natural world. Home and family are central to these joyful celebrations.

Two very significant developments occurred in the middle of the 20th century. Owing to the horrors of the Nazi policy to exterminate Jews, six million Jewish people were murdered in the Second World War. Shortly after these events, the modern State of Israel was established in 1948. Israel is seen as the homeland God promised the Jewish people.

Jews live in many countries around the world. 292,000 live in the UK (concentrated in London, Manchester and Leeds). To find out how British families across the Jewish spectrum combine ancient beliefs and teachings with modern living in the twenty-first century, read on!

1.1 There is Only One God

Learning Objectives

In this unit you will:

- analyse the impact on Jewish people of belief in one God
- evaluate the Jewish belief in an invisible God
- reflect on the impacts of belief in an all-loving God.

Starter

- With a partner, note down all the words, phrases or stories about Jewish beliefs and way of life that you already know.

Judaism takes its belief in one God and His attributes from the **Torah**. The **Shema** is a central prayer calling for belief in one God (and is said at least twice a day by observant Jews). God is believed to be all-powerful, all-present, all-knowing and all-loving.

Because the name of God is so highly regarded, many Jewish people avoid writing it out in full, in case it's damaged or erased. Instead of writing 'God', they might write 'G–d'. Jews use a number of different words for God, including Hashem (meaning 'the Name') and Adonai (often said in prayer and meaning 'my Lord'). For Jews, as with Muslims, it is not acceptable to create any visual image of God.

Useful Words

Orthodox Keeping to faith rules and traditions in a strict way

Shema Central Jewish prayer that affirms the belief in one God, and also promotes living a moral life both at home and in the wider world.

Synagogue Jewish place of worship; also a place of learning and a community centre

Torah Judaism's central text; comprises the Five Books of Moses and contains Jewish history and laws

Case Study

The Reznik family is from South Africa, but they have lived in London for a long time. They are a Modern Orthodox family, who follow a traditional Jewish way of life, and are active members of their local **Orthodox synagogue**. Modern Orthodox Judaism is a branch of Judaism which believes that traditional observance can be reconciled with participation in the modern world.

'Hear O Israel, the Lord is our God, the Lord alone.'
A quotation from the Shema

a Mr and Mrs Reznik, with their daughter Laurie and sons, Jordan and Adam.

The Reznik family explain their beliefs about God:

God is all-powerful; God is all-knowing. There's nothing God does not know. God also loves everyone. Those three things would encapsulate my belief in God. He existed before time and He'll carry on existing post-time. How do we know there's one God? For me, it breaks down into faith and logic. Faith — the Torah and our rabbis teach us. And logic — if there are two Gods, then one is not all-powerful.

I believe that everything we have is from God. He is trying to show His love for us by giving us all these wonderful things.

He's there at the good times; He's there at the bad times but He's always there to protect us. We also believe that what He does is for our good — whether good or bad.

God is not a physical being. God defies all laws of physical nature.

Activities

1. Having considered these beliefs about God, make a list of four interesting questions, one for each member of the Reznik family.

2. Mr Reznik finds the idea of there being more than one God illogical. Why might this be so?

3. In a medium of your choice, use Mr Reznik's comments about God's attributes to produce a creative response. Include your own opinions as well as the Jewish view, and ensure that you do not depict God in image form.

4. Why does Jordan Reznik say there are no physical elements to God? How might it be possible to believe in something that is invisible? Share your thoughts with a partner. Consider the idea that we cannot see love or friendship, but people still believe they exist — could something like this be possible for a being such as God?

Reflection

What might the impact be of a belief in an all-loving God?

1.2 How Does it Feel to be a Chosen People?

Learning Objectives

In this unit you will:

- examine teachings from the Torah which describe the Jews as specially chosen by God
- analyse the impact on Jews and non-Jews of the Jewish belief that they are a chosen people
- reflect on whether you have a special reason for being in the world.

According to sacred texts, God says that the **Israelites** will be a 'light to the nations' (Isaiah 49:6). In Deuteronomy 14:2 the Israelites are described as God's 'treasured people'. Exodus 19:6 says that they will be 'a kingdom of priests and a holy nation'.

For Jews, the belief that they are God's chosen people goes back thousands of years (to the time of Abram). Abram has a special importance for Jewish people – he is sometimes known as a **Patriarch** of the Jewish nation. Abram's name was later changed by God to Abraham (meaning 'father of multitudes').

> 'He took him [Abram] outside, and said, "Look toward heaven and count the stars, if you are able to count them." And He added, "So shall your offspring be".'
> Genesis 15:5

> 'On that day the Lord made a **covenant** with Abram, saying, "To your offspring I assign this land, from the river of Egypt to the great river, the river Euphrates".'
> Genesis 15:18

a

? How do you think Abram might have felt when he heard God's promise that his descendants would be as many as the stars in the sky?

Sometimes the belief that the Jews are the chosen people is misunderstood by non-Jews. Jewish people do not believe they are better than others, but that they have a special relationship with God, and an obligation to behave righteously. Jewish sacred texts say that God wanted them to be role-models for how humanity should live (according to principles of righteousness, justice and compassion towards others). The idea of being chosen is given different emphasis according to **Movements in Judaism**.

I believe that every people [...] and [...] every individual is chosen or destined for some distinct purpose. Maybe the Greeks were chosen for their unique contributions to art and philosophy, the Romans for their services in law and government, the British for bringing parliamentary rule into the world. [...] The Jews were chosen by God to be [...] the pioneers of religion and morality; that was and is their national purpose.

b Rabbi Lord Immanuel Jakobovits (former **Chief Rabbi** of Modern Orthodox Judaism), who died in 1999.

? How could the belief that Jewish people have been specially chosen by God impact non-Jews?

Reflection

Do you think everyone has special qualities and is 'chosen' for some purpose in life? Explain your reasons.

Activities

1. In pairs, take it in turns to hot-seat Rabbi Lord Immanuel Jakobovits. Use the information above to prepare questions to ask Lord Jakobovits in a TV or radio interview about what it means to modern Jews to be a chosen people.

2. From what you have learned in this unit, summarize three different ways of understanding what it means to be chosen.

3. What is your destiny and purpose? Discuss with a partner each other's strengths and skills, and decide on your answers together.

1.3 Covenants: Making a Deal With God

Learning Objectives

In this unit you will:

- explore the significance of the word 'covenant' to Jewish people
- identify four key people who made covenants with God
- reflect on the importance of signs to seal agreements.

Starter

- Have you ever made an agreement or promise? What was it?
- Now take turns with a partner to make an agreement in the form of: 'I will ... if you will ...'

A 'covenant' can be defined as a promise, contract or agreement. Something is required, or expected, in return for an agreement or promise. Often these relationships or contracts are sealed with a sign, symbol or gesture – like drinking a toast or shaking hands.

For Jews, the covenants made between God and humanity were marked by signs. God made Himself known to the Jewish people in ways that have been written down in various sacred texts. These stories are told vividly in the Torah:

- God made the first covenant with the whole of humanity through Adam – promising the wonders of creation in return for caring for the world (Genesis 1:26–30).

- One of the most important covenants in the Torah is found in the story of Noah (Genesis 9:9–17). God sent a flood to punish humanity for its wickedness, and the only people saved were Noah and his family. After the flood, God made a covenant with Noah that, if his descendants continued to live righteously, God would never send another flood. God then made a rainbow as a sign of their covenant. Some Jews believe the story of Noah actually happened, while others believe the story is a metaphor for how Jews should live and behave.

> 'I have set My bow in the clouds [...] as a sign of the covenant'
>
> Genesis 9:13

? Why might signs be used to seal agreements? What do you think the significance of the sign of a rainbow to seal the covenant with Noah might be?

a

- God commanded Abraham to leave behind his old life and show faith. The agreement was marked by **circumcision** of new-born sons. In return, he was promised specific land and also that his descendants would be a great nation – as many as the 'stars of the sky' (Genesis 15:5).

- Later on, when the Jewish people were slaves in Egypt, God made another covenant with them. He appeared to Moses and promised to rescue the people and take them to the Promised Land (see Unit 1.4). In return, they were to observe the Torah (Exodus 20:2–14).

? Adam, Noah, Abraham and Moses are important characters in the development of Judaism because they entered into covenants with God on behalf of many people. Research each one and explain who they were and why they were important (using no more than 50 words for each).

Useful Words

Circumcision The removal of the foreskin of male babies (usually at the age of eight days), by a specially trained person.

Reflection

How important are outward signs when making promises and agreements?

Activities

1 Analyse one of the covenant stories mentioned in this unit. Identify the key features of the story that show 'the covenant'.

2 Create a collage or stained glass window to explore the story of Noah and the covenant, as symbolized by the rainbow.

3 Tell a partner what you understand by the phrase to 'seal agreements'. Share examples of ways you have done this.

4 In pairs or threes, discuss the two statements below and consider your responses to them:
a 'I think it was appalling that God killed all those animals and people in the flood.'
b 'The story of the flood comes from the experience of catastrophe in life, and the comforting hope that God has promised to stand by His people.'

Learning Objectives

In this unit you will:

- examine the significance of the **Promised Land** to Jewish people
- consider the particular importance of Jerusalem to Jewish people
- reflect on the importance of special places to a faith and an individual.

It sounds delicious – a land flowing with milk and honey; a country where everything grows abundantly and food is plentiful. It was an inviting promise to the Israelites (a small wandering tribe without a settled homeland). So God made a covenant with them – they would have the fertile land of **Canaan** (see the map opposite), in return for loyalty and obedience to one God. Canaan was the old name for the land promised to the Israelites.

However, the Israelites were **exiled** from their land by the Babylonians and the Romans (1900 and 2600 years ago). From that time on, returning to the land God promised their ancestors (Abraham and Moses, for example) was an aim and a dream. Many Jewish people believe this dream was realized with the creation of the State of Israel in 1948 (see Unit 5.5).

> 'When I bring them into the land flowing with milk and honey […]'
> Deuteronomy 31:20

> 'Walk in my ways and be blameless […] this is my covenant with you […] I assign the land […] to you and your offspring […] all the land of Canaan, as an everlasting holding. I will be their God.'
> Genesis 17:1–8

a Israel – an abundant land.

? Look closely at the passages above. What does the promise show about God's relationship with the Jewish people? What do you think the dream of finding a land 'flowing with milk and honey' actually means?

b The ancient Near East at the time of the Torah.

Useful Words

BCE Before the Common Era, meaning before Year 1 in the Western calendar
Canaan Area described in the Hebrew Bible, roughly corresponding to the land of Israel
Exiled Sent away permanently
King Solomon Son of King David and builder of the first Temple in Jerusalem; known for his wisdom, power and wealth
Promised Land The Land of Israel promised to the Jews by God
Sacrifices Offerings to God of wine and grain, or animals; later replaced by prayer

Faiths have places sacred to them where God appeared and people gathered together. In the tenth century **BCE**, **King Solomon** built a Temple in Jerusalem (the capital of modern-day Israel). Here, Jews gave thanks to God by offering animal **sacrifices** and gifts of crops, although prayer later replaced the sacrifices. Jerusalem in the Promised Land has come to be of great significance to the Jewish people as a place where the presence of God may be felt.

? Find out where modern-day Israel is, and the names of the neighbouring countries. Then compare the map above with your modern map. What are the main differences?

Reflection

How and why might a place be significant to a faith? Do you have a special place? Why is it special?

Activities

1. Before the Israelites arrived, the land of Canaan already had a number of tribal groups living there in small, fortified settlements. What problems do you think the arrival of the Jews might have caused?

2. What challenges did the Jewish people face in keeping their faith in a promise that might not come true for a long time? Write two short diary entries:

   a One from the point of view of a Jew with a very strong faith in the purpose of God.
   b One from the point of view of a Jew who has doubts.

3. 'Everyone should have a dream for the future, even if it seems an impossible dream.' Do you agree or disagree with this statement? Give your reasons.

Learning Objectives

In this unit you will:

- examine the Orthodox belief in a leader, or Mashiach (Messiah), bringing about a perfect world
- consider what is needed to create a Messianic Age
- reflect on the chances of ever achieving a perfect world.

When Orthodox Jews talk about the Mashiach, they mean a special leader chosen by God to bring about a perfect world – the Messianic Age. Judaism looks forward to a blissful future for the world – with peace, love and goodness as a way of life for all living creatures. Orthodox Jews believe that the Mashiach, or 'Anointed One', will present himself as the leader for this Age.

References in sacred texts describe the Mashiach as a righteous judge, an observant Jew, and a military leader. Some Orthodox Jews say that he will arrive when the Jewish people live righteously. Others say he will come after a great and terrible battle. The Progressive Movement, however, places less emphasis on the coming of the Mashiach. Liberal Jews, and many Reform Jews, do not believe there will be a 'chosen one', but rather that each person has a responsibility to create a better world. Progressive Jews look forward to a Messianic Age rather than focusing on the Mashiach.

> '… they shall beat their swords into ploughshares, and their spears into pruning hooks: nation shall not take up sword against nation, they shall never again know war.'
> Isaiah 2:4

> 'when you will remove abominations from the Earth [...] when the world will be perfected under the sovereignty of the Almighty [...] and the Earth's wicked will all turn to you'
> Aleinu Prayer

? Look up any words in this passage that you don't understand. What does 'when the world will be perfected' mean to you?

a Tree of Life sculpture made from weapons.

How can a perfect world be created? Jewish sacred texts talk about the need to improve. Some Jews believe that if the Jewish people behave as a 'light to the nations' (a righteous example), it will lead to the healing of the world – **tikkun olam**. Sacred texts use vivid images to describe the Messianic Age, when the world will be free from wickedness (see the quotation below).

b 'Peace' painted by William Strutt in 1896.

Useful Words

Aleinu Key prayer towards the end of each religious service; describes a better world to come

Tikkun olam Repairing the world through carrying out mitzvot; it indicates the belief that humanity shares responsibility with its creator

'The wolf shall dwell with the lamb, the leopard lie down with the kid [...] with a little boy to herd them.'

Isaiah 11:6

Reflection

Do you think the world could ever be perfect, as described in this unit? Would you want it to be? What might prevent it?

? How might it feel to be living your life expecting and hoping for a better time?

Activities

1 **a** Create a mind-map showing the qualities that the Mashiach must have, according to the Orthodox view.

b Use your mind-map to help you prepare an advertisement for the job of Mashiach.

2 In image **a**, something beautiful (a sculpture) has been made out of something harmful (weapons). In pairs discuss other ideas for creating good out of bad.

3 Compare your responses to the three statements below with those of a partner:
- 'Life is "nasty, brutish and short" and any hope that it will improve is sheer fantasy.'
- 'We need to have hope in a better future, because a sense of hopelessness makes life not worth living.'
- 'Change can happen – sometimes events can happen in life which bring about a better experience.'

Chapter 1 Assessment
What do Jews Believe?

Objectives

- Apply Jewish beliefs about the nature of God.
- Reflect on the challenges of a belief in the attributes of the Jewish God.

Task

Evaluate the work of God! Try to weigh up what you have learned about God, according to Jewish beliefs. Write a work appraisal for the God worshipped by Jews. It needs to include:

- personal attributes (for example, all-present)
- previous work experience (for example, creating the world)
- the ability to select able individuals to work for Him (for example, Moses)
- the achievement of aims and objectives
- the ability to forecast.

A bit of guidance ...

Using what you know, consider Jewish beliefs about God's attributes – all-present, all-loving, all-powerful, all-knowing – and what challenges they might present.

To achieve the higher levels you should show some understanding of any differences between the various Jewish Movements in relation to their interpretation of sacred texts, and also use a wide range of religious vocabulary in your answers.

Hints and tips

To help you tackle this task, you could consider the following themes:

- Only one God
- God as creator of the world
- God as promise-maker to humanity in return for being worshipped
- God's covenants
- The Mashiach and the Messianic Age

Guidance

What level are you aiming for? Have a look at the grid below to see what you need to do to achieve that level. What would you need to do to improve your work?

	I can...
Level 3	• describe key features of God's attributes, according to Jewish beliefs • make links between these beliefs and sacred texts • reflect on the impact these beliefs have on the lives of observant Jews.
Level 4	• reflect on Jewish beliefs about God's attributes and the role of the sacred text, the Torah • use developing vocabulary to describe what I know • explain the practices in Judaism that express the belief in one God and His attributes.
Level 5	• use an increasingly wide religious vocabulary to explain the impact of Jewish beliefs on individuals and the Jewish community • make links between the role of religious sources and how they might provide answers to religious enquiry about God • recognize the differences between Jewish Movements.
Level 6	• interpret the religious and philosophical impacts of belief in one God and His attributes • give explanations for how these beliefs might influence behaviour of individuals and communities • evaluate the impacts of a range of beliefs within Jewish Movements.

Ready for more?

When you have completed this task, you can also work on your skills for Levels 6 and 7, and perhaps even higher. This is an extension task.

In small groups, prepare a collaborative piece of writing using the following question:

• If God is all-loving, why do bad things happen to people?

In order to strengthen your writing, conduct a survey around the school and present the findings in a bar chart along with your analysis.

Learning Objectives

In this unit you will:

- analyse the significance of the Torah for Jewish people
- learn how Jewish people show love and respect for the Torah
- reflect on what makes the Torah special.

Starter

- Jordan Reznik says the Torah is a 'book given by Hashem [God]. It has everything in it.' Is it possible for all the guidance you need in life to come from one book?

Case Study

Orthodox Jews, such as Jordan Reznik and his family (see Unit 1.1), believe that the Written Law of the Torah was 'dictated to Moses by God, and the Oral Law was written by **rabbis** over a period of time'. The Torah contains The Five Books of Moses: Genesis, Exodus, Leviticus, Numbers and Deuteronomy.

Jordan says that 'when we read the Written Law in shul [synagogue], it is in a scroll. It is permitted to be made into a book for home'. Jewish people show great love and respect for the Torah by covering it in a decorative mantle and storing it in an **Ark** in the synagogue.

Jordan's father says that Jews also show respect for the Torah 'by carrying out and living by the commandments'. When called to read from the Torah scroll (Sefer Torah), the word on the scroll is touched by the prayer shawl (tallit), or prayer book (siddur), and this is then kissed. The community must not turn their backs on the Sefer Torah in synagogue. Mr Reznik says that 'when it is lifted up, people stand in deference to the Torah'. (There is even a custom that, if the Sefer Torah is dropped, people must fast for 40 days!)

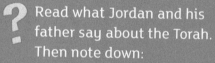

? Read what Jordan and his father say about the Torah. Then note down:
- something interesting
- something surprising
- something you'd like to know more about.

a

Case Study

As members of the **Reform** Movement, the Morris family believes the Torah is a text inspired by God but set down by humanity.

There is a saying: "Turn it and turn it for everything is in it." [...] the Torah really is the cornerstone of Jewish teaching and practice. It is the central text [...] at the base of everything we do as Jews [...] One way of looking at it is that the Torah was given to Moses and is the direct word of God. As Reform Jews, we don't necessarily interpret it like that. I could hold the position that it is a really important Jewish text, and the basis of my faith, without needing to say it came from high above.

Identify the differences between the views of the Modern Orthodox Reznik family and those of Shuli Morris, a Reform Jew.

I don't always think of the Torah as (just) a Jewish book. There are very good stories in it.

Shifra says that she likes the stories in the Torah. What examples can you give of stories you know in the Torah?

Useful Words

Ark The focal point of a synagogue; a holy cupboard containing Torah scrolls

Rabbi An ordained Jewish teacher; often the religious leader of a synagogue or Jewish community

Reform Judaism One of the Movements within Progressive Judaism which values the traditions but emphasizes flexibility, individual choice and interpretation in living a Jewish life in modern society

Reflection

What makes the Torah different and more special for Jewish people than other books? What books are special in your life and why?

Activities

1 There is a proverb which talks of the Torah as '...a tree of life to those who grasp her...' (Proverbs 3:18). Discuss with a partner what it might mean to call the Torah 'a tree of life'.

2 Create a poster with Dos and Don'ts for a Jewish family that outlines how they should behave towards the Sefer Torah.

3 Mr Reznik says that 'If we try to send an email without the dots in the right place, it wouldn't be delivered. The Torah is instruction on where we put the dots in our lives.' What do you think about this? What puts the dots in your life?

Learning Objectives

In this unit you will:

- analyse the significance of mitzvot (commandments) for Jewish people
- learn how these commandments can be interpreted by different Movements in Judaism
- reflect on the role and importance of rules in daily life.

Starter

- Take turns with a partner to list actions that are either right or wrong.
- How did you both decide what was right or wrong?

There are 613 mitzvot – commandments or rules – in the Torah (although many refer to Temple times and sacrifices that often don't apply today). The mitzvot affect everything that Jewish people do – from waking in the morning to eating, relationships and most other areas of life. **Progressive** Jews interpret the mitzvot in ways they consider relevant to modern life. Orthodox Jews believe that the mitzvot were given directly by God and cannot be changed. They observe them more strictly, according to **Talmudic** interpretations. Amongst the many categories of mitzvot, three that are very important are the commandments:

- between people and God
- between people
- between people and the world God gave.

? What kinds of rules might you expect to be related to each of these three categories? See if you can find examples from stories in the Torah.

Case Study

The Torah is very specific and quite clear on what to do and what not to do. The rules that the Torah gives govern our everyday lives in so many different ways. Moshe [Moses] brought down the Ten Commandments from the Mountain and Hashem [God] dictated to Moshe the 613 mitzvot. A concept some people look at is that the 613 rules are derived from the Ten Commandments. It's just like playing football – it would be chaos if you didn't have rules. All rules are important – every single mitzvah.

If you see rules as restrictions, it's very negative. If you see them as guidelines about how you live your life, that makes it seem a lot less hard to do.

Case Study

Hollie Walton lives in Hertfordshire. Her family are active members of their local **Liberal** synagogue, where the focus is on making Judaism relevant to modern society.

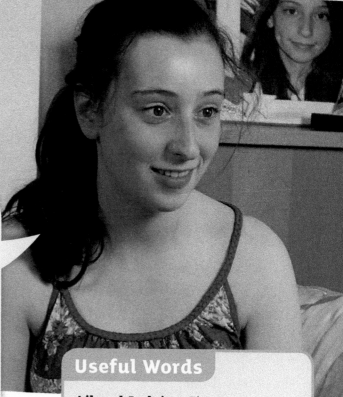

I decide what's right or wrong by what's moral – where the boundaries are in society as well as in Liberal Judaism. I keep the mitzvot that are relevant today. I don't keep the ones that aren't, because some have very vague explanations and are not relevant to our time. There's a mitzvah to sacrifice animals to God that doesn't apply today, and we don't do that. I don't really feel that restricted. I know where my boundaries lie. It's mainly my choice and whatever rules I want to follow I can follow.

? What have you learned from Laurie, Jordan and Hollie about different attitudes to mitzvot in Liberal and Orthodox Judaism?

Useful Words

Liberal Judaism The most progressive Movement within Judaism

Progressive Judaism This term includes all Movements within Judaism which have modernized, adapted or reinterpreted Jewish law (e.g Masorti, Reform, Liberal)

Talmud The first writing down of the Oral Torah (Mishnah), and commentary and interpretation of it (Gemara); a guide to Jewish law

Activities

1 Hollie Walton says: 'whatever rules I want to follow I can follow', though not all Progressive Jews would agree with her. Do you agree with Hollie's approach to rules? What would you ask her if you could? Discuss with a partner.

2 Conduct research on mitzvot and write 'A Day in the Life Of ...' for an Orthodox Jewish person, including all the mitzvot to be followed.

3 Write creatively (using prose, poetry or dialogue) about an imaginary world without any rules. Would this world be enjoyable to live in? Why or why not?

Reflection

How important are rules in daily life? Can there be too many rules? Or too few? Be prepared to justify your opinions.

2.3 Nevi'im: Prophetic Stories, Warnings and Promises

Learning Objectives

In this unit you will:

- identify the range of literature in Nevi'im and why they are important
- evaluate the significance of prophetic stories, warnings and promises
- reflect on, and respond to, a story from Nevi'im.

Starter

- In pairs, discuss a story that has made you think or taught you a lesson.

Warnings, promises and stories! The Jewish sacred text, the Tanakh, is rich in all these forms. The word 'Tanakh' is constructed from the names of its three sections:

- The 'T' from Torah
- The 'N' from Nevi'im (Prophets)
- The 'K' from Ketuvim (Writings) (see Unit 2.4).

Nevi'im is the second section of the Tanakh. It contains books with stories about the history of the Israelites once they arrived in the Promised Land of Canaan. This includes the words of **prophets**, who were believed to have communicated directly with God.

The prophets include Isaiah, Jeremiah, Ezekiel, and 12 minor prophets (including Jonah). Often, they gave warnings about historical events, and predictions about their outcomes. The prophets also spoke out against the abuse of power; reminded people to treat one another well; and called for faith in God at challenging and difficult times.

Useful Words

Prophets Seers or spokespeople transmitting messages from God

Yom Kippur The Day of Atonement (eighth day after Rosh Hashanah); a solemn fast day when Jews reflect, pray and repent for their wrongdoing during the year

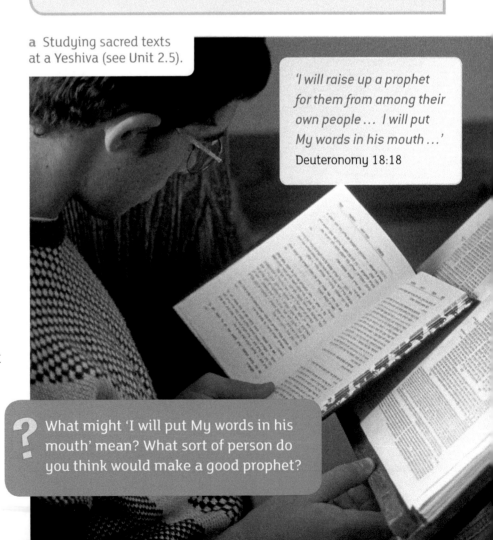

a Studying sacred texts at a Yeshiva (see Unit 2.5).

'I will raise up a prophet for them from among their own people … I will put My words in his mouth …'
Deuteronomy 18:18

? What might 'I will put My words in his mouth' mean? What sort of person do you think would make a good prophet?

A Prophet's Story – Jonah and the Big Fish!

The story of Jonah is read on **Yom Kippur**, when the central theme is God's willingness to forgive those who repent.

God commands Jonah to judge the wickedness of the people of Nineveh. However, Jonah resists God's command and runs away to board a ship. God then whips up a great storm and the ship's crew throw Jonah overboard, hoping to please God and be shown mercy.

A big fish swallows Jonah and he remains in its belly for three days and nights. Jonah repents for his disobedience to God: 'When my life was ebbing away, I called the Lord to mind' (Jonah 2:8). God commands the big fish to spit Jonah out onto dry land.

Jonah then calls on the people of Nineveh to repent for their wickedness. Eventually, in spite of his conflict with God, Jonah becomes a prophet who turns the entire population of Nineveh to God.

How effective are stories, poetry and music when sending messages? What do you think are the key messages in the story of Jonah?

Reflection

Why do you think some people 'remember' God in times of trouble?

Activities

1. In light of the Jonah story above, choose one of the following philosophical questions and discuss it in a group of three or four. See if you can arrive at several different interesting responses.
   - Does it matter whether Jonah was really swallowed by a big fish?
   - Do you think God was justified in forcing Jonah to change his mind?
   - What might the impact be of surviving frightening and difficult experiences?

2. Write a speech from Jonah to the people of Nineveh, after surviving the storm and being swallowed by the big fish, encouraging them to follow God. Reflect on how Jonah might have expressed himself differently if he had made the speech before surviving the difficult experiences.

3. In what situations could the story of Jonah be an encouragement or a challenge to a Jewish person? Discuss your ideas with a partner.

Learning Objectives

In this unit you will:

- identify the range of literature in Ketuvim
- consider the idea of Ketuvim being divinely inspired
- reflect on, and respond to, a particular Psalm from Ketuvim.

Starter

- In pairs, think of a poem or song that has moved you or made you think.
- Share whether or not you enjoy poetry. Discuss reasons for your response.

Ketuvim (Writings) are full of stories, poetry and songs. They form the third and final section of the Tanakh (after the Torah and Nevi'im). Ketuvim include:

- poetic songs (Psalms)
- wise sayings (Proverbs)
- stories of great faith in the face of difficulty (e.g. the Book of Job).

They also include Five Scrolls (**Megillot**). The writings in Ketuvim are believed to have been produced under divine or prophetic inspiration (**Ruach Hakodesh**). They have a poetic quality that may help to lift people to a higher spiritual plane.

King David is believed to have written the majority of the 150 Psalms. He was not only a musician and poet, but also a warrior (known for his famous battle with Goliath when he was young). David ruled for 40 years between around 1010 and 970 BCE. His son, Solomon, built the Temple in Jerusalem. Orthodox Judaism teaches that the Messiah, when he comes, will be a descendant of King David.

Useful Words

Megillot Five Scrolls (Song of Songs, Ruth, Lamentations, Ecclesiastes, Esther); contained in Ketuvim, the third section of the Tenakh
Ruach Hakodesh Words or messages inspired by God

a King David playing a harp, from the Westminster Psalter, circa 1200.

The book of Ruth is a story from Ketuvim. During a time of famine, a woman named Naomi is left alone after her husband and two sons have died. She urges her widowed daughter-in-law, Ruth, to return to her own homeland. Ruth tells Naomi, '…wherever you go, I will go; […] your people shall be my people and your God, my God' (Ruth 1:16). To support herself and Naomi, Ruth goes to the fields to glean. Boaz, the owner of the field, is kind to Ruth because he has heard of her loyalty to Naomi. Boaz and Ruth marry, and one of their descendants is King David.

b

> I turn my eyes to the mountains;
> from where will my help come?
> My help comes from the Lord,
> maker of heaven and earth.
> He will not let your foot give way;
> your guardian will not slumber;
> See, the guardian of Israel
> neither slumbers nor sleeps!
> The Lord is your guardian,
> the Lord is your protection
> at your right hand.
> By day the sun will not strike you,
> nor the moon by night.
> The Lord will guard you from all harm;
> He will guard your life.
> The Lord will guard your going and coming
> now and forever.
>
> Psalm 121 from Ketuvim

> 'If your enemy falls, do not exult; If he trips, let your heart not rejoice …'
> Proverbs 24:17

Reflection

What does it mean when writings are described as 'divinely inspired'?

Activities

1 Research the life of King David and create a fact file for him.

2 Either choose a small section of Psalm 121, or the story of Ruth, and:

  a explore its message in a creative form of your choice (painting, mime, writing)

  b note down how it might affect a modern Jewish person

  c note down any interesting questions that you have.

3 Use the Proverb on this page to devise a role-play with a partner acting out the message in a modern setting.

2.5 The Talmud: A Guidebook for Jewish Living

Learning Objectives

In this unit you will:

- explain the form and role of the Talmud
- evaluate the impact of the Talmud on Jewish life today
- reflect on who or what you turn to when something is hard to understand.

Starter

- What is a guidebook? When might you need one?

So many sacred books ... so many words! Orthodox Judaism believes that God communicated with Moses in two different ways. The **Written Torah** and the **Oral Torah** were both given to Moses 3500 years ago on Mount Sinai. The Written Torah is recorded in the Five Books of Moses, but it is more difficult to keep track of the Oral Torah. When the Jews were exiled and scattered throughout the world, Rabbis feared that the word-of-mouth tradition would be lost. They, therefore, wrote down the Oral Law in the Talmud.

The Talmud's recording of the oral laws is like a guidebook that helps to explain and interpret the written Torah. The Talmud covers all aspects of living, such as: prayer, family life, sacrifices and personal purity. It is divided into two parts:

- The Mishnah contains the Oral Law (divided into six books).
- The Gemara is a more-detailed interpretation of the Oral Law.

Orthodox men, young and old, study the Torah and Talmud in a place of learning called Yeshiva, where they try to understand how God really wanted Jewish people to live.

Within the Progressive Movement men and women study together. Many Progressive Jews view the Talmud as an inspiration, which sparks debate on complex problems. They accept that individuals may come to different conclusions.

Useful Words

Oral Torah Words that Orthodox Jews believe were spoken by God to Moses, and then written down much later in the Talmud

Shabbat Day commemorating the creation of the world, when God rested on the seventh day; it begins at sunset every Friday and ends at nightfall on Saturday

Written Torah The Five Books of Moses

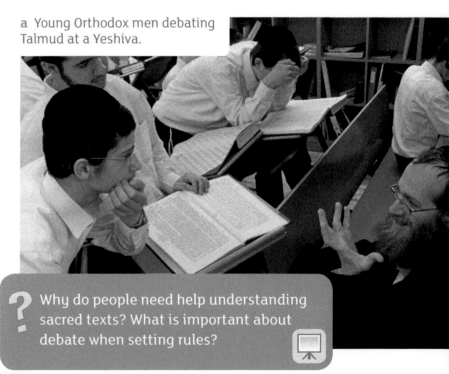

a Young Orthodox men debating Talmud at a Yeshiva.

? Why do people need help understanding sacred texts? What is important about debate when setting rules?

? Progressive Jews choose to keep Shabbat in ways that are meaningful to them and not necessarily in accordance with the laws of the Talmud. Is it a good idea to modernize ancient rules? Why or why not?

The Reznik family celebrate Shabbat in accordance with the Torah, and are also careful to follow the way the Talmud interprets these laws (see quotations below).

A verse from the Torah about keeping **Shabbat** *rules:*

'Remember the sabbath day and keep it holy. Six days you shall labour [...] but the seventh day is a sabbath of the Lord your God: you shall not do any work – you, your son or daughter, your male or female slave, or your cattle, or the stranger who is within your settlements.'

Exodus 20:8

The Talmud interprets the Torah text:

What does the Torah mean by 'work'? Chapter 7 of the Mishnah in the Talmud interprets 39 acts of work. Just a few of these are: 'no sowing or ploughing; no stitching; hunting; writing; building or demolishing; making or putting out a fire'.

Activities

1 In a group of two or three, discuss what you think counts as work today. Using a flipchart, make two mind-maps on different sheets – one with 'work' in the centre and one with 'not work'. Fill in your ideas about work. How are they the same or different from the interpretation given in the Talmud?

2 Devise a questionnaire to find out other people's opinions about what counts as work.

Reflection

What or who do you turn to when something is hard to understand?

Produce statements or questions that allow an Agree or Disagree response.

3 'The Talmud is an ancient text and does not apply to modern Jewish people.' Debate this statement in small groups.

2.6 Passover: Why is This Night Different From All Other Nights?

Learning Objectives

In this unit we will:

- explore the story of the first Pesach (Passover)
- analyse the role and importance of the Hagadah at the Pesach Seder
- reflect on the importance of freedom for yourself and others.

Starters

- Discuss with a partner stories that have been important to you, and explain why.

The spring festival of Pesach (Passover) recalls that God forced the Egyptians to release the Jews (who were their slaves), by sending ten plagues to Egypt. The Torah commands the Jewish people to tell their children the story of the escape from Egyptian slavery.

There is great excitement in Jewish households before Pesach! Here, some Jewish families share their feelings about the festival.

Nina Morris says that Pesach involves 'incredibly high levels of preparation, because it's based in the house [...] scrubbing out corners of your cupboards [to remove leaven], making foods without flour or yeast.'

'And you shall explain to your son on that day, "It is because of what the Lord did for me when I went free from Egypt".'
Exodus 13:8

a In the Exodus story, the angel of death 'passed over' the homes of the Jewish people – who had marked their doorposts with the blood of a lamb. In Egyptian homes (without marked doorposts), the angel of death killed every firstborn child.

? You may already know something about Moses and the escape of the Jews from Egypt. Read Exodus 12 as a reminder.

b Symbolic foods are laid out on the Seder table (explained in the Hagadah) – matzah (baked bread that has not had time to rise), maror (a bitter herb to represent the pain of slavery), pesach (a bone recalling the Jewish sacrifice of lambs before they fled), and salt water to represent tears.

Many Jews believe that celebrating Pesach and remembering these events is something that they must pass on to future generations. Children in the family play an important part in the ritual. Family and friends gather in each other's homes for a Seder (an evening service and meal, where the Pesach story is told from a book called the Hagadah). The story, songs, blessings – and eating a festive meal – create a joyful atmosphere.

My favourite Hagadah goes into deeper meaning and tells me more interesting facts.

This Hagadah would have been on my parents' table. One of the good reasons for having different Hagadahs, rather than being repetitive, is that they bring a different thought, a different picture and elicit a different meaning.

The Hagadah contains four questions, beginning with: 'Why is this night different from all other nights?' The youngest child in the family traditionally asks the four questions. On this night, Jews remember, not only their freedom from slavery in Egypt, but also other experiences of persecution so that they can remember the hardships their ancestors endured.

Reflection

A central theme of Pesach is freedom. Why might freedom be important to Jewish people? What freedoms do you value?

Activities

1. In pairs, devise a simple story or pop-up book to explain to young children the importance of the Pesach story and its celebration.

2. Research the four questions that Jewish children ask at the Seder service. Then, with a partner, devise a series of images (one for each of the four questions) to depict the answers that would be given.

3. Mr Reznik says Pesach is 'a conversation across generations'. Why is it important for history and traditions to be passed on from generation to generation? Give reasons.

2.7 Judaism in a Changing World: What do the Rabbis Say?

Learning Objectives

In this unit you will:

- examine the views of **rabbis** from different Movements in interpreting Jewish law and practice
- respond to people from different Jewish Movements
- reflect on the idea of spiritual honesty.

Starter

- In pairs, discuss examples of when you have interpreted something in a different way from others. How do you decide which is the 'right' way?

Rabbis have a long tradition of immersing themselves in the study of the Torah. They constantly question and debate matters of Jewish law and practice. Over time, many rabbis have influenced changes in interpretation and practice in different directions to adapt to the modern world. This has resulted in the development of different Movements within Judaism.

- Ultra-Orthodox Jewish people believe that the 613 mitzvot in the Torah were given directly from God, and that humanity cannot change them.
- Modern Orthodox Jews believe it is possible to participate in modern society whilst strictly observing Jewish law but recognize that modern life requires its careful interpretation. For example, many work for non-Jewish companies which are happy to accommodate their need to leave early for Shabbat in winter, or take Jewish festivals as holiday.
- The Progressive Jewish Movement (including Masorti, Reform and Liberal Judaism) broke away from strictly Orthodox interpretations of the Torah in the nineteenth and twentieth centuries. They believe in focusing on what is meaningful to Jewish people living in a modern, multi-faith and multicultural environment. They give individuals greater choice over which mitzvot they decide to follow.

a Lord Jonathan Sacks, Chief Rabbi until 2013. The Chief Rabbi is selected by the United Hebrew Congregations – the mainstream Orthodox Jewish Movement. He is a high-profile figure, and influences how other faiths, and the secular world, view mainstream Orthodox Judaism.

b Rabbi Julia Neuberger was the first woman to be rabbi of her own synagogue in the UK and President of Liberal Judaism. She was created a Life Peer as Baroness Neuberger in 2004. She is now Senior Rabbi at a Reform synagogue, and as another high-profile figure, she has the power to influence the ways in which people think about Judaism from a Progressive point of view. She embodies a flexible and egalitarian approach to Judaism.

Liberal Judaism was established because we are trying to integrate traditions that can be applied today – but not follow laws that cannot. In Liberal Judaism, we consider the role of women as having the same importance as the role of men. Women are integrated into the synagogue, can lead services and become rabbis.

I think the idea of changing Jewish law and practice to reflect a modern world is at the heart of the ethos of Reform Judaism, which is about reconciling living our life in modern society as an integrated member of that society and Jewish **Halakhah**, Jewish law and practice.

Mr Morris, Shuli's father, describes how his female rabbi believes that 'you should do something wholeheartedly in the spirit of the law, rather than grudgingly or reluctantly observing the letter of the law'. For Reform Jews 'it is about observance and spiritual honesty'.

Useful Words

Rabbi An ordained Jewish teacher; often the religious leader of a synagogue or Jewish community
Halakhah Hebrew for 'the way'; Jewish code of conduct affecting every aspect of living

Activities

1. In a small group, research the views of *one* of the rabbis from this unit, or from other Jewish Movements: Rabbi Louis Jacobs, Rabbi Hugo Gryn, Rabbi Schneerson, Maimonides. How do they interpret Jewish law and practice? Present your findings as a class presentation.

2. Prepare questions to hot-seat a student playing the role of an Orthodox rabbi. Repeat for a rabbi from one of the Progressive Jewish Movements.

3. Prepare your response for a debate on the statement: 'If you don't adapt ancient rules for modern times, people will stop following the religion.'

Reflection

Mr Morris talks about 'spiritual honesty'. What do you think that means?

Where do Jewish Beliefs Come From?

Objectives

- Explore the nature of key Jewish sacred texts.
- Evaluate the role of sacred texts in Judaism.
- Assess the impacts of those sacred texts on Jewish beliefs.

Task

Become teachers for a day! In pairs, prepare a 20-minute lesson about the Torah. It should aim to be understandable and enjoyable for students who know very little about Judaism. Be creative! Use a range of resources and teaching methods to enable your audience to engage fully with the learning experience.

A bit of guidance...

Decide in advance on your target audience.

Keep the language lively and engaging, and try to imagine what might be most useful and interesting for students to discover about the Torah.

To achieve higher levels, show understanding of how sacred texts are interpreted in different Movements within Judaism, and use a wide range of religious vocabulary in your answers.

Hints and tips

To help you tackle this task, you could consider the following themes:

- The Torah as a book and a scroll
- Written in Hebrew
- Believed by Orthodox Jews to be the word of God
- Contains the Five Books of Moses
- Interpreted in the Oral Law of the Talmud

Guidance

What level are you aiming for? Have a look at the grid below to see what you need to do to achieve that level. What would you need to do to improve your work?

	I can...
Level 3	• describe a key Jewish sacred text • make links between its role in Jewish worship and daily life • reflect on the impact of the Torah on Jewish people.
Level 4	• use religious vocabulary to describe and show understanding of the role of a sacred text in Judaism • raise questions and suggest answers about the nature of a sacred text and how it is used in Judaism • make links between Jewish practices and worship and the Torah.
Level 5	• evaluate the role of the Torah in Judaism, giving clear reasons and examples (using developing religious vocabulary) • ask questions and suggest answers to what is expressed in a Jewish sacred text about history, belief and practice • recognize how Jewish Movements interpret knowledge, belief and learning from a sacred text differently.
Level 6	• analyse the impact of a sacred text on the practice of Judaism, using religious and philosophical vocabulary • raise questions and suggest answers about where religious history, belief and knowledge come from, relating it to my own life and that of others • evaluate the different ways Jewish Movements interpret the Torah, with reference to the Talmud.

Ready for more?

When you have completed this task, you can also work on your skills for Levels 6 and 7, and perhaps even higher. This is an extension task.

Compare the ways in which sacred texts are valued and interpreted in Judaism with what you have learned about sacred texts in another faith you have studied.

Learning Objectives

In this unit you will:

- explain the origins of Shabbat (Sabbath) and the ceremonies that are involved
- compare the observance of Shabbat in Orthodox and Progressive Jewish Movements
- reflect on the value of creating a 'space in time' in your own life.

Starter

- Jewish Shabbat observance involves refraining from work on Saturdays. What would you do on a day without work?

The creation story in the Torah says that God created the world in six days and then rested. As a result, there is a commandment to keep Shabbat as a holy day free from work.

- Shabbat begins on Friday night with candles being lit in the home and a blessing being said. Kiddush, before the evening meal, is a brief ceremony of blessings over wine to sanctify the day. Before the meal, everyone washes their hands and says the blessing which is said before any meal, with another blessing said over two specially baked, plaited loaves, called challot. These are placed under a decorative cloth.
- The end of Shabbat is marked on Saturday evening with another ceremony, called Havdalah.

> 'Remember the sabbath day and keep it holy.'
> Exodus 20:8

Mrs Reznik and Laurie light Shabbat candles.

Case Study

Mr Reznik of the Orthodox Jewish Movement describes welcoming Shabbat as 'a wonderful mystical feeling; you can actually feel the calmness coming over you'.

Orthodox Jewish people do not work, drive, use technology, cook, carry, or write on Shabbat. Part of the day is spent in synagogue and sharing meals prepared the day before with family and friends.

? Research the Havdalah ceremony. What happens, and what does it symbolize?

The Rezniks make Havdalah to mark the end of Shabbat.

Case Study

Shuli Morris says that for her, Shabbat is not about the strict observance of rules.

Shuli says: 'We do use technology, which as Reform Jews, is not what "working" signifies for us. It is about "making a holy space in time", by refraining from what makes the rest of the week a time for work. It really is a special time for all of us.'

? What do you think Shuli Morris means by Shabbat being 'a holy space in time'? How is Jack Walton's Shabbat different from that of the Reznik family?

Nina says: 'We try to take advantage of the day. We spend more time together. We don't do homework on Shabbat. It makes it really different from the rest of the week. I really look forward to it.'

[In the Liberal Jewish Movement] we celebrate Shabbat at synagogue, where we have a Friday night service with singing and prayers. At home, we have a family meal and catch up. Shabbat is about the family and community, which is what makes Shabbat special – not the laws and customs. We don't really follow that many laws that apply for Shabbat, like not using electrical appliances.

Reflection

Would you like to create a 'space in time' in your own life? What might you do in one rest day a week to make it special?

Activities

1. With a partner, devise a tag-line that captures the essence of Shabbat for all Movements in Judaism.

2. Make a list of well-known board-games/ games/activities which would not break the laws of Shabbat in an Orthodox Jewish household.

3. Form debating teams to consider the statement: 'A day of rest from all work is a good idea'.

3.2 Let's Think Food

Learning Objectives

In this unit you will:

- explain and evaluate the significance of Jewish food laws
- analyse the impact of kosher eating on Jewish people's sense of community
- reflect on the possible impacts of following certain food rules.

Starter

- What are your five favourite foods? Share and compare with a partner.
- Are there foods that most people don't eat? Why?

Religious beliefs affect all aspects of Jewish people's lives – even the food they eat and how it's prepared. Special food laws, called **Kashrut**, tell them what food is allowed (kosher) and what is not (non-kosher). In Orthodox households, milk and meat must be kept separate and cannot be eaten in the same meal.

? From what Mrs Reznik and Laurie have said, which foods are non-kosher?

Case Study

The Reznik family are Modern Orthodox Jews. They live in a London neighbourhood with many other Jewish people. The Rezniks observe the Jewish dietary laws closely, believing them to be commandments from God.

The way the animal is slaughtered is under strict supervision. We eat meat from kosher animals (those with **split hooves** that **chew the cud**). So, an animal like a cow is permitted, but an animal such as a pig is not, because – although it has split hooves – it does not chew the cud. We eat meat that is specially prepared and it is **kashered**. All the blood is drained out of the meat before we buy it. The fish we eat is only fish with fins and scales. We make sure we don't eat blood because blood is a part of life.

Laurie says: 'All rules are important about food: keeping milk and meat separate; buying food that has a stamp that says it's kosher; making sure you check fruit and vegetables so there are no bugs. There are quite a lot of kosher shops where we live, and also supermarkets like Tesco have a kosher section. Some foods that don't come from kosher companies are still kosher.'

Mrs Reznik and Laurie cooking in their kosher kitchen.

The practice of avoiding eating milk and meat in the same meal – and having separate cooking utensils, cutlery and crockery – is a Talmudic interpretation of the line in the Torah: 'You shall not boil a kid in its mother's milk' (Exodus 34:26). The way in which animals are slaughtered, and the avoidance of eating blood are included in the 613 mitzvot.

- Orthodox Jewish people keep the dietary rules strictly. This means they may not be able to go to some restaurants, or buy at all food shops – and usually cannot eat at the homes of non-Jews. This binds them more closely to God's laws and the Jewish community. Some believe it strengthens their Jewish identity.

- Progressive Jewish people adopt a more flexible approach to dietary laws. Reform Judaism recognizes the value of some dietary rules and that for many Jews Kashrut is an essential part of their connection to God. However, it needs to be combined with ethical behaviour. Some Liberal Jewish people regard the rules of Kashrut as less relevant, whilst others choose to obey at least some of them as a significant part of Jewish tradition.

Useful Words

Chewing the cud The process by ruminants (mammals like cattle, goats and sheep) of regurgitating plant matter from the first stomach to be chewed again

Kasher To purge blood from meat by using salt in order to make it kosher

Kashrut Jewish dietary laws and practices

Split hooves Hooves that divide down the middle, e.g. those of a goat or cow

a Jewish Delicatessen selling only kosher food and meat.

Reflection

If you had to consider rules that didn't allow you to eat certain foods or combinations of foods, what differences do you think it would make to your life?

Activities

1 Think of two reasons why it might be difficult for an Orthodox Jewish person to eat in a non-Jewish person's house.

2 Where does the Jewish idea of separating meat and milk products come from?

3 What have you discovered from the text about kosher meat? Divide a page in half. On one side, write examples of food that is kosher, and on the other side non-kosher. Create a logo for each category to appear on packaging.

4 In pairs, create an attractive menu card for a three course kosher meal. What rules will you need to remember?

5 Form teams to debate the statement: 'It's nearly impossible for people to keep kosher rules in modern society.'

Learning Objectives

In this unit you will:

- explore the importance of synagogues for Jewish people
- identify and explain the key features of synagogues
- evaluate the communal activities in your own life.

Starter

- Look at these images of items in a synagogue and find out what they are. How do you think they are treated by worshippers?

A synagogue, or 'shul', is a meeting place where Jewish people gather together regularly for worship and other activities. The synagogue's main room is used for prayer, but there are other rooms used for study, meetings and social activities.

The main feature of the synagogue is the **Aron Hakodesh**, or **Holy Ark**. In front of the Ark burns an everlasting light (the Ner Tamid), which symbolizes the presence of God and reminds Jews of the lamp that burned at all times in the Temple in Jerusalem. During worship on some mornings, the Torah scrolls are taken from the Ark to a raised platform (the Bimah).

The Torah (see Unit 2.1) is treated with great love and respect. It is 'dressed' in a beautiful mantle and adorned with a silver breastplate. When the Torah is read, the parchment is not touched, to avoid damaging it. Instead, the Hebrew words are followed using a **yad**.

? How can you tell that the Torah is the most important feature of a synagogue? How do Jewish people show their love and respect for the Torah?

Synagogues are much more than places of worship. They provide a range of different activities including cheder (children's Hebrew classes), nursery schools, clubs and venues for celebrations.

- In Orthodox synagogues, three services take place at different times of day: morning prayer (Shacharit); afternoon (Mincha); and evening (Ma'ariv). Saturday morning (Shabbat) is the most popular time to attend – when prayer is usually led by the rabbi, the **chazan**, or members of the community, and there is reading from the Sefer Torah. Women and older girls sit in a gallery separate from the men. Orthodox synagogues use only the Hebrew language in services.

- Progressive synagogues tend not to hold three prayer services a day – concentrating more on Shabbat and festivals. They pray in both English and Hebrew. Men and women sit together and women may lead services, read from the Torah, give sermons and participate in exactly the same way as men.

> **?** What differences can you identify between Orthodox and Progressive worship in the synagogue?

e Interior of an Orthodox synagogue – the New West End in London.

Useful Words

Aron Hakodesh/Holy Ark
The focal point of a synagogue; a holy cupboard containing the Torah scrolls
Chazan Leader of reading, singing and chanting in the services of some synagogues
Yad A pointer, in the shape of a hand, used when reading the Torah

Reflection

You come to school to learn, meet with friends and get involved in other activities. Which aspects of this communal activity are most important for you, and why?

Activities

1. Write as if you were a Torah scroll, telling small children – in a way they would understand – about your different parts and how you like to be treated.

2. Create an eye-catching poster advertising a week's activities for either an Orthodox or a Progressive synagogue, including prayer services. You could research a local synagogue online to find out more.

3. Look at the different images in this unit. Using your knowledge of Judaism so far, consider in what ways these objects and meeting places are important for Jewish people.

Learning Objectives

In this unit you will:

- explain the significance of some Jewish festivals
- evaluate the importance of festivals for the Jewish community
- reflect on your own experiences of festivals and celebrations.

Starter

- Which festivals mark different stages of the year for you? Are they religious, secular, or a mixture of the two?

The Jewish year includes many festivals with historical, Biblical and seasonal significance. The pilgrim festivals – Pesach (see Unit 2.6), **Shavuot** and **Sukkot** (see Unit 3.5) – were when Jews would go to the Temple in Jerusalem to make a sacrifice. Nowadays they are celebrated in the home, which plays a key role, but there are also synagogue services or community events for each festival.

? Why do you think people mark and celebrate different times of the year?

Case Study

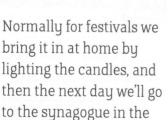

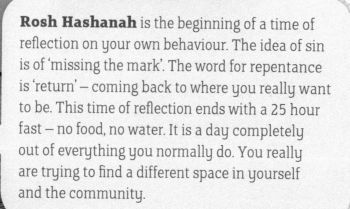

Normally for festivals we bring it in at home by lighting the candles, and then the next day we'll go to the synagogue in the morning.

My favourite festival is Shavuot. You read the Book of Ruth. She is a powerful role-model for someone who is not a born Jew. One of Ruth's descendants is King David, so there is an open door. Jewish texts are extremely rich and they really draw you into a relationship with the religion, whatever your starting point.

Rosh Hashanah is the beginning of a time of reflection on your own behaviour. The idea of sin is of 'missing the mark'. The word for repentance is 'return' – coming back to where you really want to be. This time of reflection ends with a 25 hour fast – no food, no water. It is a day completely out of everything you normally do. You really are trying to find a different space in yourself and the community.

Case Study

Jack Walton says: 'I like **Purim**, because we all dress up at school. We have a fair and give money to charity and have fun.'

Mr Walton says: 'I like **Simchat Torah** best. We celebrate the end of the cycle of reading from the Torah. Everyone dances round the synagogue. We unravel the Torah scroll, which is the most amazing sight. Normally, you only see snippets of it unfurled.'

Reflection

What have you enjoyed and valued most about festivals and celebrations that you've taken part in at home, school, in the community, or elsewhere?

Useful Words

Purim A festival commemorating the rescue of Persian Jews; the story is told in the Book of Esther

Rosh Hashanah The Hebrew words for 'head of the year'; Jewish New Year celebrated in autumn

Secular Without religious reference; non-religious

Shavuot The Hebrew word for 'weeks'; one of the three pilgrim festivals celebrated seven weeks after Pesach (Passover); it commemorates the giving of the Torah

Simchat Torah An autumn festival celebrating the completion of the year's cycle of Torah reading (celebrated with much joy and dancing with Torah scrolls)

Sukkot A pilgrim festival celebrated in autumn, when temporary dwellings are built to commemorate the Jews wandering homeless in the wilderness

Activities

1. With a partner, research more about Jewish festivals and produce a calendar of the times when they occur.

2. Choose one of the festivals mentioned in this unit and research it in more detail to create a festival fact sheet.

3. Use your fact sheet work from Activity 2 to identify key beliefs, rituals and practices, and how these link to what you have already learned about Judaism so far.

4. In a small group, choose one of the Jewish festivals and prepare a creative workshop to teach its different elements to young children. Include arts and crafts activities and the preparation of suitable food as part of the workshop.

3.5 Sukkot: A Festival of Joy

Learning Objectives

In this unit you will:

- explore the Jewish festival of Sukkot in more detail
- analyse the impact of celebrating Sukkot
- reflect on the use of symbols in the festival of Sukkot.

Starter

- How do you think it might feel to have no permanent home?

Sukkot is an autumn harvest festival which reminds Jewish people of a time when their ancestors were wandering in the wilderness after the exodus (see Unit 1.3) without a permanent home. Some Jewish families build a temporary structure, called a sukkah, outside their house, and take all their meals in it for eight days. This is a reminder of the 'booths' or temporary huts that the Jews built as shelter when they were a nomadic people. Eating or living in the sukkah also reminds Jewish people to be thankful for what they have, and to keep material values in perspective.

> **?** Why do you think Jordan Reznik describes Sukkot as 'the happiest festival of the year'?

Case Study

We come to Sukkot, the happiest festival of the year, following a time of regret and asking God for forgiveness. We have our Four Species (**lulav**), a wand made from willow, myrtle, palm, and the fruit of the citron tree (etrog). The ritual of 'shaking the lulav' is carried out during the synagogue festival service and at home in the sukkah.

The lulav is symbolic in a number of ways. It can represent the different types of Jewish people – the willow represents people who only learn the Torah; the myrtle leaves represent people who only do mitzvot; and the etrog represents both people. Another way of thinking about the lulav is that it contains symbols of parts of the body – the etrog is the heart and is sweet; the myrtle leaves look like the shape of the lips; the palm is like the spine; and the willow is like the eyes.

There is also a tradition of remembering Jewish biblical characters. We [symbolically invite] these characters [**ushpizin**] to eat [with us] in our sukkah. Often there are drawings of them by children to decorate the sukkah.

Jordan shows a photo of a sukkah he built.

a

? Why does building a sukkah remind Jewish people of a time in their history?

b

Useful Words

Lulav Palm wand used as part of the Four Species during Sukkot

Ushpizin The Aramaic word for 'guests'; the tradition of symbolically inviting spiritual ancestors, like Abraham and Isaac, to the sukkah

? Which type of Jewish people does Jordan say the Four Species in the lulav represent?

Activities

1 Imagine you have been invited to Jordan's house to celebrate Sukkot. What do you imagine would happen? What would you be looking forward to?

2 In what ways does Sukkot link with the experience of refugees and homeless people? Write creatively on this theme, using poetry, prose, dialogue, or a journal entry.

3 What symbols are used in the celebration of Sukkot? How do they help Jewish people to understand the meaning of the festival?

Reflection

What reminds you to be thankful for what you have? In what ways could you try to keep material values in perspective?

Learning Objectives

In this unit you will:

- examine what the Torah says about rules for day-to-day clothing
- learn about the meanings behind Jewish religious garments
- reflect on the possible impacts of wearing religious garments in a multicultural society.

Starter

- What do you think the unit title means, and do you agree that 'You Are What You Wear'?

Who we are and what we believe may be expressed in how we choose to present ourselves to the world through our clothing. The Torah influences everyday clothing for Jewish men and women – not just religious garments:

- Modesty (tzniut) is a central value in Judaism, as expressed in Micah 6:8: 'to walk humbly with your God'. Orthodox Jewish women are expected to dress modestly, in sober colours – with their legs, collarbones, and arms above the elbow covered. After marriage, some Orthodox women also cover their heads with a scarf, hat or even a wig (called a sheitel).

- A small proportion of Jewish men (ultra-Orthodox or Charedim) wear only black clothing with black hats.

- Leviticus 19:19 forbids any clothing made from a mixture of wool and linen: 'you shall not put on cloth from a mixture of two kinds of material'. This perhaps reflects the importance of purity and of 'being one thing' – the principle of shatnez – and echoes the belief in only one God.

There is a far more relaxed attitude towards day-to-day clothing within Jewish Progressive Movements, and modern styles and fashions are worn by both men and women.

? What do modesty and humility mean? See if you can give a definition for each. How do Jewish people show modesty and humility in the way they dress?

a Orthodox and modern day-to-day dress.

The Torah also has a lot to say about Jewish religious garments as they are spiritual aids to focus the mind for prayer:

- Deuteronomy 6:4–9 teaches that God's commandments should be bound 'as a sign on your hand and let them serve as a symbol on your forehead'. The Talmud interprets this through the practice of 'laying tefillin' as part of morning prayers on weekdays. Tefillin are two small leather boxes with thongs for the hand and the head.

- The tallit is a fringed prayer shawl worn every day for morning prayers. The strands and knots add up to the number of commandments in the Torah – 613! From the age of three, Orthodox Jewish males wear an undergarment with fringes, called tzizit. Both the tallit and the tzizit are an interpretation of Numbers 15:37–41.

- A more common sight is the wearing of a kippah (sometimes called a yamulkah or capel). This is a small skullcap to remind Jews that 'the Divine presence is always over my head' (Talmud).

b A young Jewish man prays wearing tefillin and kippah.

Activities

1. In what ways do people show their values through what they wear? In pairs, discuss your favourite outfit. Why do you like it and what does it say about you?

2. How do Jewish people interpret the commandments in sacred texts about what they should wear?

3. What advice would you give to someone who has been invited to visit the home of an Orthodox Jewish family about what they should wear to show respect?

4. Why do you think that many Jews who belong to Progressive Jewish Movements have a more relaxed attitude towards their clothing? Discuss your thoughts with a partner.

5. Prepare and discuss your responses to these two statements:
   - 'People should keep symbolic clothing for home and places of worship, but in public life we should not be confronted by religious symbols.'
   - 'An individual should be free to express religious identity in choice of clothing.'

c Bar Mitzvah boys wearing a tallit for the first time.

Reflection

Think about Judaism and other faiths you have studied. What are the possible impacts of wearing religious garments in a modern multicultural society?

Learning Objectives

In this unit you will:

- explain how life-stages are marked in Judaism
- evaluate real experiences of Jewish rituals and celebrations
- reflect on your views about celebrating life-stages.

Starter

- Do you agree people should celebrate major life-stages? Have you ever celebrated a life-stage event?

Case Study

Nina and Shuli Morris (from the Jewish Reform Movement) explain different Jewish life-stages, and what the Jewish community does to respond to them:

Judaism gives you a marriage ceremony, and there is a given ceremony for when you become **Bar** and **Bat Mitzvah**. Judaism also tells you what to say when someone dies. It is very good at making sure the community supports mourners, and there are systems to make sure the grieving family is well looked after – cooking food for them, for example.

As a religion, Judaism really focuses on those important times, and integrates itself into the rhythm of human life. When a boy is born they have **brit milah**, which is particular to boys when they are eight days old. At a Bar or Bat Mitzvah, they wish you a life of Torah, **huppah** and **ma'asim tovim**. I think that's a good tag-line! In a Reform Jewish Bar or Bat Mitzvah there is no difference between what we [girls] did and what a boy in our community would do. We both read from the Torah. We received a prayer shawl – a tallit. You wear it as an adult. The first time you wear it is at your Bar or Bat Mitzvah.

? Write down the different stages of human life from birth to death. What do you think Shuli Morris means when she says Judaism 'integrates itself into the rhythm of human life'? Give examples of how other faiths celebrate or mark the human life cycle.

Case Study

There is great excitement about the planning of Bar and Bat Mitzvah coming-of-age ceremonies within Jewish communities. Jordan and Laurie Reznik explain what happens in Orthodox Judaism:

Useful Words

Bar Mitzvah A Jewish boy's coming of age at 13 years old
Bat Mitzvah A Jewish girl's coming of age at 12 or 13 years old
Brit milah Circumcision
Daven Recite prayers
Haftarah Passages from Nevi'im (Prophets)
Huppah A wedding canopy, symbolizing the marital home
Ma'asim tovim Good deeds

A Bar Mitzvah is when boys turn 13. They become obligated to do the mitzvot they were not obligated to before. Currently I am taking lessons. On your Bar Mitzvah day, you chant from the Torah and then you read from the **Haftarah**. After Bar Mitzvah, I can go to shul [synagogue] with my father and, instead of being in the background, I can **daven**.

A girl, when she turns 12, becomes Bat Mitzvah. I did a different preparation from Jordan. I said a speech called a D'var Torah (words of Torah) instead of reading from the Torah. We had a celebration with my family and friends from all over.

? What is the difference in attitude to Bar and Bat Mitzvah in different Jewish Movements?

Reflection

Which event on the journey of life do you think is the most important? Explain why.

Activities

1 What obligations might a Jewish young person have after their Bar or Bat Mitzvah? Create a mind-map with a partner.

2 What would be the impact of Bar or Bat Mitzvah? Write a reflection or poem on how you imagine it might affect a 12 or 13 year old.

3 Which statement below do you agree with most and why?
- 'Marking occasions adds hugely to the enjoyment of life.'
- 'There's no point in marking life occasions. Life goes on regardless.'

Belonging to the Jewish Faith

Objectives

- Consider how Jewish people live day-to-day.
- Apply your knowledge about Judaism reflectively.
- Analyse the diversity in religious expression across the range of Jewish Movements.

Task

Choose three of the most significant facts that you have discovered about living day-to-day as a Jew. Write a magazine article explaining these for a target audience of young people who know nothing at all about Judaism. Write in a lively and interesting style.

A bit of guidance...

Explain any Hebrew or useful words in brackets as you go along.

To achieve the higher levels, you should show some understanding of any differences between the various Jewish movements in relation to your chosen themes, and also use a wide range of religious vocabulary in your answers.

Hints and tips

To help you tackle this task, you could consider some of the following themes:

- Dietary laws
- Shabbat observance
- Festivals
- Religious dress and what it means
- How life-stages are marked
- Sacred texts

Guidance

What level are you aiming at? Have a look at the grid below to see what you need to do to achieve that level. What would you need to do to improve your work?

	I can...
Level 3	• describe some key features of Judaism • ask questions about what is involved in belonging to the Jewish faith • reflect on my own responses to answers.
Level 4	• show understanding of what it means to belong to the Jewish faith • explain how belonging to the Jewish faith impacts daily life • support answers with evidence.
Level 5	• explain, using a wide range of religious vocabulary, the impact of belonging to the Jewish faith on individuals and communities • make relevant links to my own life and experiences • ask questions and suggest answers about different interpretations of sacred texts which impact on how Jewish people express their Judaism.
Level 6	• use religious and philosophical language to evaluate the practice of Judaism • analyse the effect of different Movements within the Jewish faith, and how they express their sense of belonging • analyse, using arguments and examples, how belonging to a faith group, such as Judaism, impacts on people's sense of history and identity.

Ready for more?

When you have completed this task, you can also work on your skills for Levels 6 and 7, and perhaps even higher. This is an extension task.

Choose a theme from the hints and tips section that you did not write about in your article.

• Prepare a speech that includes a PowerPoint presentation aimed at conveying information and stimulating discussion. You could also include artefacts or outside speakers. Be inventive!

• Create a practical exercise which will help the audience to understand the topic.

• Give examples of the differences between Jewish Movements.

Learning Objectives

In this unit you will:

- examine Judaism's beliefs about the value of human life and of living well
- learn how these beliefs are expressed by Jewish people
- reflect on your own attitude to the value of life.

Case Study

The Jewish view is that the sanctity and quality of life are very, very important. We are against anything to do with killing or losing a life. We are not allowed to harm or kill ourselves or have tattoos or harm the body in any way. It says in the Talmud that saving a life is the same as saving the whole world, which shows that one life is of the same importance as a whole group of people.

At any excuse, we are eating together, drinking together, wishing each other well. At different times of year we get together for festivals. It's a very happy religion – very joyous.

We feel Hashem [God] gave us life – it's the biggest gift you can give a person. We are taught to treasure each day. At simchas [celebrations] and festivals, it's a tradition when we drink to say 'L'Chaim'. It means 'To Life!' Let's celebrate for now because it means so much to all of us to enjoy life.

Judaism is a very joyous religion, because we have survived so many situations and we have come out stronger.

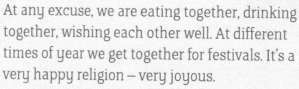

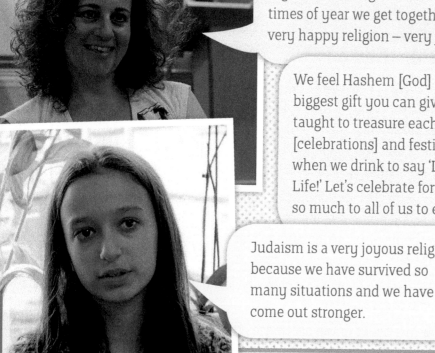

The Reznik and Walton families have talked about how important valuing and preserving human life are to Judaism. Life is far more important to Judaism than thinking about what happens beyond. Even in death, life is affirmed. The first foods a mourner traditionally eats, following the funeral, are circular – an egg and a bagel – reminders of the circular and continuous nature of life. There are many opportunities during Shabbat, festivals and life cycle events to celebrate life joyfully. A joyful celebration is called a simcha, from the Hebrew word for joy. Blessings are said frequently to show appreciation for life.

> *'I have put before you life and death, blessing and curse. Choose life...'*
> Deuteronomy 30:19

? Try to sum up in a sentence the Jewish view of human life. Should human life be saved at all costs? How do Jewish people demonstrate the joy of living?

a Simcha dancing at a celebration

Reflection

Mrs Reznik says that people should 'treasure each day'. How do you make every day count? Are her words good advice for living your life?

Activities

1 Write a journal entry for one day, focusing on how you value your own and other people's lives.

2 Create a collage with the title L'Chaim! (To Life!), showing life cycle events and how they are celebrated (photos, mementos, invitations).

3 Many people today have tattoos and piercings. Some Jews argue this shows a lack of respect for your own body. What do you think and why?

4 You are in a hot air balloon which is overweight and about to crash. Only one of these three people may remain: a scientist aged 90, a nurse, the Prime Minister. In a group of three, discuss who you would choose and why.

5 Conduct some research and choose a news broadcast. How might Jews respond to the issues raised given their beliefs about life?

Learning Objectives

In this unit you will:

- learn about the Jewish belief in an annual Day of Judgement
- consider the possible impacts of this belief on Jewish people
- reflect on beliefs about judgement and forgiveness.

Starter

- In pairs, share your experiences of doing wrong and say how you were judged.
- Take two minutes to write what comes to mind when you hear the word 'forgiveness'.

Each autumn, Jewish people celebrate the festival of Rosh Hashanah (the Jewish New Year), which is also called 'Day of Judgement'. For ten days during and after the festival – during the 'Days of Awe' – they reflect on their deeds and behaviour over the past year. It is a time when Jews believe that God weighs up a person's good deeds against their bad deeds and decides what their next year will be like.

Jewish people believe God's judgement is made on the tenth day, at Yom Kippur (a solemn day of fasting). During the Days of Awe, Jews believe that if they are truly sorry for their bad deeds (and pray and do acts of charity), God will be fair and compassionate, and they will be forgiven. There is a particular custom on Rosh Hashanah afternoon. After a long synagogue service, and lunch with family and friends, Jewish people gather by flowing water. In their pockets they carry breadcrumbs which symbolize the sins they want to throw away. They then cast the breadcrumbs into the water, which carries them away in the current. This is called Tashlikh, from the Hebrew word meaning 'casting off'.

a

> **?** Jewish people believe that prayer, acts of charity and repentance are necessary in the Days of Awe. What do you do when you are truly sorry? Do you think good deeds can help to cancel out bad ones?

b Throwing away sins by flowing water: the custom of Tashlikh.

> 'On Rosh Hashanah will be inscribed and on Yom Kippur will be sealed; how many will pass from the earth and how many will be created; who will live and who will die [...] But repentance, prayer and charity remove the evil of the decree!'
> A prayer from Rosh Hashanah Machzor (Prayer Book)

> 'You will hurl all our sins into the depths of the sea.'
> Micah 7:19

Activities

1. Think back over the last year and consider all the good or bad things you may have done. Then answer the following questions:
   - How do you think each deed would be weighed up in God's balance? Is it an easy judgement to make?
   - How does it feel to remember what you've done in the past?
   - When you start a new year do you try to start off with a resolution to be a better person?

2. Prepare your arguments for a debate about the statement: 'There are no people who are totally wicked or totally good – we all fall somewhere in-between'.

? Why do you think sins are thrown away symbolically into flowing water?

Reflection
How might beliefs about judgement and forgiveness influence people's lives?

4.3 Is Death the End?

Learning Objectives

In this unit you will:

- explain Jewish beliefs about death and the afterlife
- analyse the impacts of these beliefs on Jewish practices
- reflect on your own views about a possible afterlife.

Starter

- 'There is life after death.' Do you agree, disagree – or are you unsure?

Judaism places great emphasis on how life should be lived. It teaches that what happens next is in the hands of God. Jewish people are commanded to honour one God and live righteously, justly and compassionately amongst fellow people by carrying out the covenant and keeping God's laws.

Judaism is vague about life after death. However, the Tanakh tells of a shadowy place called Sheol (a place of waiting for the ultimate Day of Judgement, when people will be rewarded or punished by God). Traditional Judaism believes in heaven – the eternal destination of Gan Eden (The Garden of Eden) – for the good, and hell (Gehinnom) for the wicked.

There is an Orthodox belief in Techiyat Hametim (the resurrection of the dead at some future time), although this is not usually accepted by Progressive Jews. Early Biblical descriptions suggest that the soul continues to exist in some way after death. In Jewish practice and custom, it is the focus on life and the living that is most important.

? Judaism has conflicting beliefs about the afterlife. What do you think the impact of this could be?

? This is an artist's impression. What do you imagine Sheol, Gan Eden and Gehinnom to be like?

a

Judaism's emphasis on life is evident even in its response to death.

Cremation is forbidden in the Orthodox Movement, because of the belief in a physical resurrection that will require a body. However, cremation is allowed in the Progressive Movement.

There are strict rules about burial and mourning. Ideally, burial should take place within 24 hours of death. Someone will remain with the body from the time of death until burial. Coffins are plain and simple. Men are often buried in a **kittel**, and are wrapped in their tallit with the tassles cut off (because they no longer need to remember all the commandments these signify). Close family mourners at the funeral will make a small rip in their clothing to show their grief. The mourners will recite the Kaddish, or Mourner's Prayer, after the coffin is lowered into the ground.

Following the funeral, mourners return to one of the family's homes and 'sit shiva' for seven days. Shiva prayers are held each evening attended by family, friends and community. During the mourning period, the Jewish community provides food and relieves the family of mundane daily tasks. Much attention is paid to honouring the dead person, but also caring for the living mourners. To stress the central importance of life, mourners are greeted with the words 'I wish you long life'.

'May His great name be exalted and sanctified in the world which He created according to His will.'
A fragment of the Kaddish (Mourner's Prayer)

b

? How do Jewish people show care for the living in the period of mourning, and how do you think the bereaved people feel about this care?

Activities

1. Write a diary entry from the perspective of someone who has attended a Jewish funeral.

2. In a format of your choice, either visual or written, create your own response to Gan Eden, Gehinnom or Sheol.

3. Write a short explanation of how Jewish mourning rituals could help people to come to terms with death.

4. Do some research to find an obituary of a famous person (not necessarily Jewish). Analyse it to show how it celebrates life.

Reflection

Revisit your initial thoughts in response to the Starter activity in this unit. Have you changed your view? If so, why? If not, has anything strengthened your view? Explain.

Useful Words

Kittel A white robe worn by men in some synagogues during the High Holy Days; also worn by some bridegrooms and used as a burial shroud

Learning Objectives

In this unit you will:

- consider some of the challenges involved in practising Judaism in a non-Jewish society
- examine how some Jewish people deal with this issue
- reflect on your own views about 'difference'.

Starter

- In what situations do you feel 'different' from those around you? How does it make you feel?

The Walton and Morris families have described some of their experiences of being Jewish in a non-Jewish society. With Shabbat observance, festivals throughout the year (sometimes falling on working days), and keeping the Jewish dietary laws, being Jewish is not always easy in a non-Jewish world.

Orthodox Jewish people sometimes live and work together in the same communities. This might make it easier for them to keep Jewish laws and traditions. The Progressive Jewish Movement interprets some rules differently – emphasizing the spirit rather than the letter of the law. They believe this helps to make their integration into wider society less challenging.

? Why might it be positive to belong to a minority culture? What other challenges do you think there might be in observing Judaism in a non-Jewish society?

Case Study

I think there's a huge advantage to being part of [a minority group who are] not part of the mainstream, because it means you are constantly questioning. You look at things a bit more carefully. Part of being Jewish is to question. One of the first things you learn is to start off the Passover service by asking the Four Questions.

I have worked in companies where I was a minority there, but I've always seen a lot of tolerance. It hasn't always been easy to take time off for Jewish holidays. A certain match clashed with the First Night of Passover and I had a real dilemma! But I did not go to the game and I did stay at home for a Seder.

Anti-Semitism refers specifically to the persecution of Jews. It is one of many forms of prejudice and persecution against groups that are perceived to be different. Anti-Semitism, however, has a long and consistent history, partly because Jews have lived as a minority in many countries and have been regarded as outsiders.

> I think I am very fortunate to live in a country that supports minority faiths. I know people at my school who have been victims of anti-Semitism and hate, but overall I do think that England is a good country to live in.

> I think I'm really lucky. I've never had any experience of anti-Semitism, not directly.

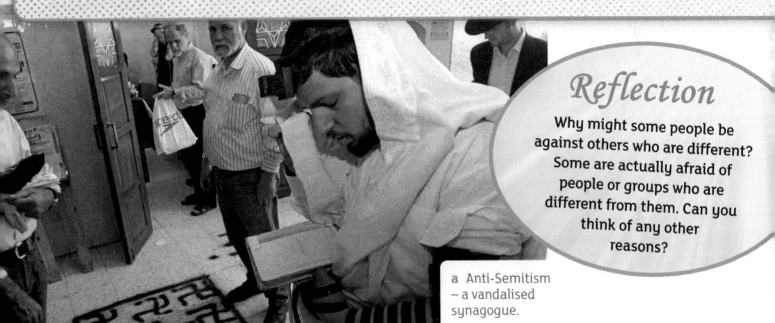

Reflection

Why might some people be against others who are different? Some are actually afraid of people or groups who are different from them. Can you think of any other reasons?

a Anti-Semitism – a vandalised synagogue.

Activities

1. Shuli and Jack mentioned anti-Semitism in their comments. Can you explain what this is in your own words?

2. In pairs or threes, create a role-play about a dilemma involving one of the following issues for an observant Jewish person living in a non-Jewish society: kashrut, modest dress, Shabbat observance, festival observance, the need to pray three times a day.

3. In pairs, create a dialogue between someone who belongs and someone who doesn't (for example, to a faith, gang or friendship group). Show what it might be like for both the insider and the outsider.

Learning Objectives

In this unit you will:

- identify the difference between natural and man-made evil
- evaluate Judaism's arguments about God and suffering
- reflect on, and respond to, the effects of the Holocaust.

Starter

- Can you name some examples of natural evil and man-made evil?

Why do innocent people suffer? Why is there evil in the world? These questions have puzzled humanity throughout time. If the Jewish God is all-powerful and all-loving, how can there be suffering and evil?

Evil is often classified in two ways:

- Natural evil, e.g. disasters caused by hurricanes, floods or earthquakes.
- Man-made evil, e.g. stealing, murder or terrorism.

Judaism believes that, within human nature, there lie both the inclination to good (yetzer hatov) and the inclination to bad (yetzer hara). As Jews believe that God made man, it can be argued that the evil inclination is part of God's creation. Some Jewish people believe that, without this evil inclination, there would be no opportunity for humanity to exercise free will in making moral and rational choices and, therefore, to grow, overcome temptation and develop a righteous character.

A key principle in Judaism is chesed (loving kindness) which, as well as the study of the Torah, can combat the evil inclination. Some rabbis believe that the good and innocent who suffer on earth will receive their reward in the world to come.

a A woman weeps after the 2004 tsunami in India: a natural evil.

b Planes collide with the World Trade Center towers in New York City in 2001: a man-made evil.

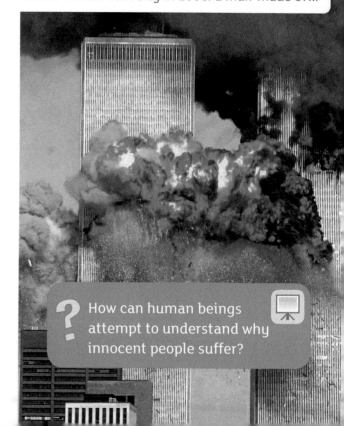

Useful Words

Genocide The deliberate extermination of a race or group

Holocaust The Nazi government's systematic extermination of six million Jews during the Second World War; often called the Shoah by Jews (meaning 'catastrophe')

Persecution Harassment, hurt or putting to death, often for religious or political reasons

? How can human beings attempt to understand why innocent people suffer?

Throughout history, examples of human evil abound. One of the most shocking man-made atrocities (the Holocaust) happened during the twentieth century. As Nazi government policy, over six million Jewish men, women and children were systematically shot, gassed, or murdered in brutal concentration camps during Nazi rule in different parts of Europe. Some Jews believe that God 'died' in Auschwitz; for others, it has strengthened their faith.

? Jews have been persecuted throughout their history, but they have survived as a people. What impact do you think this **persecution** might have had on them and their views?

Case Study

Nina Morris studied the **Holocaust** at school, and produced an artwork related to it. She explains that 'the Holocaust is much more connected to me as a Jew'.

Nina's sister, Shuli, also discusses her feelings about the Holocaust: 'That's my people and I am one of them.' Shuli believes that the Holocaust 'has huge ramifications for Jewish thought and attitudes, and is part of my Jewish consciousness'. Shuli feels that to 'remember it is so important for fighting against **genocide**. We have a responsibility as a people who have gone through this to show the world how important it is that those things don't happen [again].'

c The gates of Auschwitz Concentration Camp say 'Work makes you free' in German.

Reflection

Nina Morris found this quotation in a Holocaust victim's prayer book: 'I believe in the sun when it is not still shining; I believe in love even when feeling it not; I believe in God even when he is silent.' What does this quotation say about the Holocaust victim? How do you respond when life becomes difficult?

Activities

1 What do you think the quotation 'God died in Auschwitz' might mean?

2 How might we try to understand the suffering during the Holocaust? Use the information in this unit as a starting point.

3 Create a pocket-book devoted to acts of chesed. Create a page a day and write down an act of loving kindness that you will aim to carry out every day to help develop your yetzer hatov (inclination to good).

4 Like Nina Morris, create your own piece of artwork, or artefact, on the theme of the Holocaust.

5 'Those who stood by and did nothing are just as much to blame for the horrors of the Holocaust.' Prepare for a debate on this topic.

Learning Objectives

In this unit you will:

- examine the Jewish belief in the importance of 'stewardship' of the earth
- evaluate the Jewish contribution to environmental awareness
- reflect on personal responsibilities towards the environment.

Starter

- In pairs, give examples of how humans might destroy the environment. Then, describe how they could protect it.

In the Torah, God created a beautiful and miraculous world in just six days! He entrusted humanity to 'rule the fish of the sea, the birds of the sky, the cattle, the whole earth and all the creeping things' (Genesis 1:26). Ruling the earth on behalf of God is called 'stewardship'. To dominate the land involves taking a sacred responsibility to do so in a way that guards and protects the environment.

Jewish tradition teaches that humanity must rule the earth righteously, and treat the natural world with the utmost care and respect. To do so, humanity must put aside short-term desires and inclinations, and show discipline in using the world's resources wisely.

God gave humanity freedom of choice to consider the needs of future generations. In the twenty-first century, we are more and more aware that human influence is damaging the ecological balance of our world. The rainforests and ice caps are shrinking; natural resources from the earth and the sea are being used up; pollution is increasing; and the global climate is changing.

> '*After creating Adam, God took him round all the trees of the Garden of Eden and said to him: "See how lovely and excellent My works are; I have created them all for you. Take care not to spoil and destroy My world, for if you spoil it there will be no one to repair it after you".*'
>
> Midrash

? How would you explain the Jewish belief in humanity having 'stewardship' of the earth? Tell a partner. What would humanity need to do in order to become more responsible and righteous stewards of our planet?

a The Garden of Eden

Allowing the land to rest every seven years – a kind of Shabbat for the earth – is carried out in Israel and is called shmita (from the Hebrew word for 'release'). Planting, pruning, ploughing and harvesting are forbidden during this year. Caring for the land and its inhabitants in this way is an example of righteous and responsible stewardship.

Since it started at the beginning of the twentieth century, the Jewish National Fund (JNF) has planted over 240 million trees in Israel. It has also built 180 dams and reservoirs, developed 250,000 acres of land, and established over 1,000 parks. Other Jewish environmental campaining groups, such as The Big Green, demonstrate the commitment of Jewish people to work to improve the environment in countries outside Israel too.

> 'Six years you shall sow your land and gather in its yield; but in the seventh you shall let it rest and lie fallow. Let the needy among your people eat of it, and what they leave let the wild beasts eat. You shall do the same with your vineyards and your olive groves.'
> Exodus 23:10

Activities

1. Create a word-cloud for what might be included in 'righteous and responsible stewardship of the planet', according to Jewish belief.

2. Draw a circle and create different-sized segments within it. Then write in each segment an action that you think demonstrates care and 'stewardship' of the environment. Place in the larger segments those actions you think are particularly important.

3. Devise a role-play between a 'responsible and caring', and an 'irresponsible and selfish', steward of the planet.

Reflection

Jews believe that being entrusted by God with 'stewardship' of the environment comes with responsibilities. What responsibilities do you believe you have towards the environment?

Raising Questions, Exploring Answers

Objectives

- Explain, in the light of Jewish faith and practice, how Judaism might respond to a specific issue or dilemma from modern society.
- Reflect on your own response to the same issue.

Task

Based on what you have learned in this chapter, how do you think Orthodox Jewish people might respond to the issue of voluntary euthanasia? Write three or four paragraphs.

The specific question you have to answer for this task is: 'Euthanasia goes against Jewish belief. As an Orthodox Jew, do you agree?'

a

A bit of guidance...

Take time to reflect. Firstly, you need to decide on your own response to the issue of voluntary euthanasia. Then think about how you might respond if you were placed in the hot-seat to answer this question from the standpoint of an Orthodox Jew. Consider the question from what you know about the Orthodox Jewish position on issues of life and death. What arguments might there be for and against euthanasia? Mind-map your thoughts before writing up your response.

Hints and tips

To help you tackle this task, you could consider the following issues:

- Whether life must be preserved at all costs
- The quality of the person's life (for example if they are terminally ill, in pain and suffering)
- The wishes of the person who wants to die
- The impact on the person's loved ones, who will go on living without them
- The argument that only God can decide when human life ends
- What might happen to the soul

Guidance

What level are you aiming at? Have a look at the grid below to see what you need to do to achieve that level. What would you need to do to improve your work?

	I can...
Level 3	• describe a modern issue that confronts Judaism • use religious vocabulary when considering the Jewish response • ask questions about the Jewish response • reflect on my own response to this issue.
Level 4	• explain a modern issue that confronts Judaism, and consider the Jewish response • reflect on how the response might differ, depending on which Jewish Movement is involved • raise questions about, and suggest answers to, how different Jews might respond to the dilemma • support my answers with examples.
Level 5	• reflect on, and respond to, how Judaism might tackle a modern issue that challenges Jewish law and teachings • use a wide range of religious vocabulary • ask questions, and suggest answers, about how different interpretations of sacred texts might affect how Judaism addresses a modern issue • show understanding of the diversity of attitudes in different Jewish Movements.
Level 6	• use religious and philosophical language to evaluate the possible Jewish response to a modern issue or dilemma • integrate Jewish sources in my answer • raise and answer questions in a way that is informed by Jewish sacred texts • analyse how beliefs, informed by Jewish sacred texts, might impact on decisions about a modern issue and how Jewish people respond.

Ready for more?

When you have completed this task, you can also work on your skills for Levels 6 and 7, and perhaps even higher. This is an extension task.

Repeat the task from the standpoint of a Jewish person from the Liberal Movement. How does it compare with the Orthodox position? What are the similarities and differences?

Compare the responses of Judaism with those of members of another faith you have studied.

Learning Objectives

In this unit you will:

- identify and explain Jewish faith activities that take place at home
- evaluate the significance of home and family to Jewish identity
- reflect on the influential role of parents and carers over their children.

Starter

- What special occasions do you celebrate at home? Do you have special traditions?

The family plays a central role in Jewish life. Jewish people are encouraged to marry and have children, and home is seen as a very important place. For Jews, religion is an integral part of everyday life, and many faith activities take place at home.

'Hear, O Israel! The Lord is our God, the Lord alone. You shall love the Lord your God with all your heart and with all your soul and with all your might. Take to heart these instructions with which I charge you this day. Impress them upon your children. Recite them when you stay at home and when you are away, when you lie down and when you get up [...] Inscribe them on the doorposts of your house and on your gates.'

Deuteronomy 6:4–9

? What parts of everyday life are referred to in the Shema quotation above? How hard do you think it would be for Jews to keep God's words in their hearts and minds all the time? What difference would it make to the way they live?

a A mezuzah is a small, special box attached to the doorposts in a Jewish home. Inside the mezuzah is a prayer, the Shema, which reminds the Jewish family to love God and teach His words to their children.

Jewish festivals have their own customs and special foods, and are often celebrated at home with extended family and friends – especially Sukkot and Pesach (Passover). A central occasion is the weekly celebration of Shabbat. Each Friday night, there is a joyful service followed by a family meal at home to welcome the sabbath.

Some life cycle events are also marked at home. For example, the **circumcision** of a male baby usually takes place at home. After a death, Jewish people spend seven days of mourning (sit shiva) at home (see Unit 4.3), and the anniversary of the death of a loved one is marked by lighting a jahrzeit (memorial) candle in the house.

Jewish people may also pray at home, including on Shabbat, festivals and special ceremonies. Most Jewish homes have copies of three special books: a Siddur (book of daily prayers), a Chumash (the Torah in book form) and Machzorim (prayer books for festivals).

Reflection

What do you think is the most important lesson parents and carers can pass on to children?

Activities

1. 'Home and family are the lifeblood of Judaism.' Rewrite this statement in your own words, showing what you think it means and giving examples from what you have learned.

2. Write a mission statement for a family about passing on Judaism from generation to generation.

3. • 'We should live life according to our beliefs and principles.'
   • 'Life is full of surprise so we just have to get by any way we can.'

   Discuss your responses to these statements.

4. Using the information in this unit, design a mezuzah case as a present for a Jewish friend.

Learning Objectives

In this unit you will:

- evaluate how Jews put into practice the commandment to teach children to love and worship one God
- identify where and how Jewish learning takes place
- reflect on your own views about the impact of faith-based schools.

Imagine eating sweet food whenever you learn something! In the Middle Ages, on the first day they attended school, young children's fingers would be dipped in honey. They would then trace the first letter of the **Hebrew** alphabet on a slate. Afterwards, the children would lick the honey from their fingers to create a sweet memory of Hebrew learning.

There is a central idea that the survival of Judaism depends on passing on the faith to children. Jewish children learn about Judaism at home and many of them attend supplementary (Sunday) schools at their synagogues or youth activities, where they learn about Judaism and the Hebrew language too. Today, 60% of Jewish children attend Jewish faith-based schools, where they follow a regular curriculum and also learn about Judaism.

> 'Train a lad in the way he ought to go; He will not swerve from it even in old age.'
> Proverbs 22:6

> 'Impress them upon your children'
> Deuteronomy 6:7

> I can learn Maths from other people, but Jewish studies can only be done by people of my faith. Being at a faith-based school doesn't prevent me from learning a lot about the world.

Case Study

> Growing up, I regretted not learning Hebrew and not having the deeper roots of my religion. By sending our children to learn at this young age, it gives them the best opportunity to learn their Jewish history and to develop as strong, moral people. Jordan and my daughter, Laurie, do extra-curricular activities where they do interact with other children, and it's very important and it shows mutual respect.

Case Study

These are two different personal views on faith-based schools:

? What have you discovered about Jewish faith-based schools from Jordan and Jack? What else would you like to know?

I go to a Jewish school. It is very centred around Judaism and prayer; there are assemblies and Bar and Bat Mitzvah groups. We learn Jewish studies and **Ivrit** three times a week. We learn about Jewish history. We also have Hebrew.

Useful Words

Hebrew The language of Jewish sacred texts, written from right to left

Ivrit Modern Hebrew; the language of the State of Israel

I have some serious issues with faith-based schools. One needs to integrate into society, but the growth in the number of faith-based schools is by definition divisive. It also negatively impacts the synagogue, because young people choose not to come.

Reflection

Jordan and Jack's Jewish education is very important to them. What impacts could there be of going to school with only students who share the same belief system as you?

Activities

1. Explore the different views on faith-based schools. Begin by imagining that you are the head teacher of a Jewish faith-based school. Your job is to write the introduction to the school prospectus, with the aim of convincing Jewish parents of the advantages of sending their children to a Jewish school. Then write a letter from Rabbi Pete to parents, explaining the disadvantages.

2. From Jack Walton's account of his learning, devise a timetable for a typical school week. How does it differ from your week?

3. What makes learning and education a positive experience? Share your ideas with a partner. How can education impact on the continuation of faith?

4. • 'Faith-based schools cut children off from wider society.'
   • 'Schools should support the identity of those they serve.'

   Considering arguments for and against, write a response to these statements.

Learning Objectives

In this unit you will:

- examine the roles of men and women, and questions of sexuality, in modern Judaism
- analyse how different Jewish Movements approach these issues
- reflect on your own views about the issues raised.

Starter

- Put your thumbs up or down to show whether you think men and women have equality in today's society. Discuss reasons with a partner.

Case Study

It is really important to me that Reform Judaism promotes **egalitarianism**. I think there should be no question that men and women should be given equal rights and opportunities. In Orthodoxy, men and women have different roles. If that is how they choose to practise it, that is fine, but that would inhibit me.

We have a fantastic woman rabbi and female cantor [chazan] at our synagogue. It has been lovely for me bringing up three girls and watching them blossom with these female role-models.

Within Liberal Judaism, we believe in total equality – so there are lots of women rabbis who conduct services. [Women] are allowed to read from the Torah and face the bimah – do everything that a man would do. Liberal Judaism values all relationships. We value gay relationships. We can have gay rabbis, and have gay partnerships. It encompasses every aspect of modern society.

Traditionally, women were to look after the home and nurture the children, but this isn't in accordance with Liberal Judaism. Women take an active role in society – not just Judaism. You will see women working; it's not an unusual thing.

? What have you discovered from the Morris and Walton families about female participation in synagogue services within Progressive Jewish Movements?

Many modern issues might come into conflict with a religion that has its roots in an ancient time and place. The Morris and Walton families have just focused on the role of today's women and girls, especially in synagogue. Mrs Walton also raised the issue of homosexual relationships. Orthodox Judaism conforms to the Biblical ban on homosexuality (Leviticus 18:22). However, the Progressive Movement takes a different stance and is more open to homosexual relationships.

Modern Orthodox Jews believe that women can play a part in contemporary society. While many Orthodox women focus on traditional roles of home-making and raising a family, others have successful careers and occupy management positions on synagogue boards and within Jewish organizations. Women are considered equal to men, but men and women often have different roles.

b An Orthodox woman.

a Rabbi Miriam Berger from Finchley Reform Synagogue, where the Morris family attend.

Reflection

Where can young people, whether they are religious or not, go for advice about dilemmas in relationships?

Activities

1. Use the information in this unit to plan your arguments for a debate about the statement: 'Judaism needs to adapt to meet the needs of Jewish women living in the twenty-first century'.

2. Imagine that you are the Agony Aunt or Uncle for a magazine. What advice would you give to a young Jewish person who is either gay or lesbian and concerned about how their religious community might react to their sexuality?

3. Imagine that you are about to interview a young Jewish couple who are planning to marry. Plan some questions to explore their views about the different roles of men and women and the issue of 'different but equal'.

5.4 Why is Charity Important?

Learning Objectives

In this unit you will:

- evaluate the meaning of charity (tzedaka) to Jewish people
- interpret Jewish sacred texts about charity
- reflect on and respond to the practice of giving to charity.

Starter

- Write down five groups of people who might need charity.
- How might giving to charity affect society?

Tzedaka is the Hebrew word for 'justice' or 'righteousness' and is often expressed by giving to charity. Tzedaka is a central act and obligation in Judaism, whether a person is rich or poor, and aims to make the world a fairer place.

? What is the meaning of tzedaka? What do you think Mrs Morris means when she talks about giving people a fishing-rod rather than a fish? Why is this important?

Case Study

Mrs Morris points out that, in Judaism, giving to charity (tzedaka) is not a voluntary act of generosity but a religious requirement – to make sure that the world is a fairer place.

Adam puts tzedaka in the box before we go to school on Friday. They say if you give charity, your food on Shabbat will taste even nicer!

The best form of giving is when you enable someone not to need charity any more – the idea of giving a fishing-rod, not a fish. During the Days of Awe, the High Holy Days, there is a traditional appeal. Our synagogue will maybe have four charities, two Jewish and two non-Jewish, which people will vote on.

a Jewish girls helping in a soup kitchen.

Case Study

Judaism teaches that you should give 10% of your income to charity. There's also something that's not applicable to modern-day society ... the idea that you should give a corner of your field if you are a farmer, or if you drop some of your harvest (your crop) you should leave it – not pick it up – for the poor. Judaism teaches that you should do tikkun olam, which means repairing the world for the better – and giving to charity can help the world and make it a better place.

b

? Jack Walton mentions ways of helping others besides giving money. What are they?

Reflection

Jack Walton talks about tikkun olam. How might giving to charity impact society? Can it 'repair the world'?

Activities

1. Design a tzedaka box with Jewish symbols that represent Jewish beliefs about charitable giving.

2. Devise a slogan to help persuade people to give 10% of their income to charity.

3. Create an advertisement for a charity fund-raising event at your school. You should include the charity you want to support; inform people of how you want to support it; and explain why they should become involved.

4. Read Jack Walton's comments about the traditional harvest charity. How might this be applied to modern times? Write a new teaching that would bring it up-to-date.

5.5 The State of Israel: The Promised Land

Learning Objectives

In this unit you will:

- learn about events in the history of the Jews, leading to the establishment of modern-day Israel
- analyse the importance of the State of Israel to Jewish people
- reflect on the issue of Jerusalem's significance to different faiths.

Starter

- Which country do you feel you belong to and why? Does anyone in the class feel loyal to more than one country?

There is a belief in Judaism that Jews are a people chosen by God (see Unit 1.2), and that the land now called Israel is the land promised to them by God thousands of years ago. However, for almost two thousand years, most Jewish people were exiled from this land (see Unit 1.4). Throughout their exile, they prayed and hoped to be able to return to the promised land.

Jews have been persecuted throughout their history. The terrible events of the Holocaust (Shoah) in the Second World War (see Unit 4.5) was a tragedy that continues to affect them deeply.

In 1947, the United Nations (set up after the Second World War) agreed to share the land known as Palestine between the Jews and Arabs who lived there. The State of Israel was established formally in 1948. For Jews, this meant that they could live and worship freely in their own country. Under the Law of Return, any Jewish person from anywhere in the world has the right to settle in Israel.

However, modern Israel has come into conflict with its neighbours, and also the Muslim Arabs who lived in Palestine before the Jewish State was established. There have been several wars since 1948, and disputes about Arab and Israeli rights to the land continue. The land of Israel – and particularly the city of Jerusalem – has great religious significance for the three major world faiths of Judaism, Christianity and Islam. This issue continues to cause conflicts.

> **?** How might a history of persecution affect Jewish attitudes to having a homeland? Discuss with a partner some possible effects of the Law of Return.

a Jewish Independence Day celebrations in Israel – waving the Israeli flag.

Case Study

Many Jewish people from all over the world feel a strong connection to Israel. They may visit often, or even 'make aliyah', which is when families or individuals decide to settle and make a new life in Israel. Here are two different attitudes to Israel from the Morris family.

> I don't feel that connected to Israel. I feel I would want to help people suffering in any country in the world, just as much as people in Israel.

> I think I have very complicated feelings about Israel. I feel it is a part of what I have inherited as part of my religion. I did visit Israel last year and it was a meaningful experience for me to go to the Kotel [Western Wall of the ancient Temple in Jerusalem] ... because it's been a gathering point for people of my faith throughout the ages. I think of it differently from my attitude to England.

? Why might Shuli Morris have 'complicated feelings' towards Israel? Compare the two sisters' attitudes to Israel.

b Jerusalem, Israel.

Reflection

What would a perfect multi-faith city be like?

Activities

1. Research with a partner five new facts about the State of Israel. Create a five-minute presentation.

2. Do some research to find out why Jerusalem is so significant to members of three major world faiths. What important events have taken place there?

3. What are the challenges for the three faith communities in living in a shared city? How might they work for peaceful co-existence?

4. Use the following words to try and explain the situation in Israel: identity, tradition, conflict, peace.

5. Write your thoughts creatively on the subject of 'Homeland', using poetry, prose or dialogue.

Jewish Beliefs in Action

Objectives

- Reflect on how Jewish people might behave in response to their beliefs.

- Explore the actions and way of life adopted by Jews in response to their beliefs.

a

Task

How do Jewish people behave in response to their beliefs? Write an essay which focuses on five Jewish beliefs. Each belief and corresponding response should be explained and evaluated.

A bit of guidance...

Think about how each belief might affect the behaviour of a Jewish person. For example, a Jewish person who believes in giving tzedaka might give food or money to someone who is homeless.

To achieve the higher levels, you should show some understanding of any differences between the various Jewish Movements in relation to their beliefs and responses, and also use a wide range of religious vocabulary in your answers.

Hints and tips

To help you tackle this task, you may wish to consider Jewish beliefs about:

- home and family
- education
- the role of women and men
- charity
- a homeland

Guidance

What level are you aiming for? Have a look at the grid below to see what you need to do to achieve that level. What would you need to do to improve your work?

	I can...
Level 3	• describe five beliefs and possible Jewish responses to them, using religious vocabulary • make links between these responses and what sacred texts say • reflect on the impact of these beliefs.
Level 4	• reflect on Jewish beliefs taken from sacred texts, and how they impact on key areas of life • use developing religious vocabulary to express knowledge • explain deeds, practices and behaviour in Judaism that are a response to belief.
Level 5	• use an increasingly wide religious vocabulary to explain responses to Jewish beliefs by individuals and the community • make links between the role of religious sources and how they are responded to by Jewish believers • recognize differences in the responses of Orthodox and Progressive Movements.
Level 6	• interpret the impact of Jewish responses to beliefs • give reasons and explanations for how responses might impact on individuals and communities, using religious and philosophical vocabulary • evaluate the significance of a wide range of beliefs within Judaism, and discuss how this might influence responses • analyse the responses to Jewish beliefs of wider society.

Ready for more?

When you have completed this task, you can also work on your skills for Levels 6 and 7, and perhaps even higher. This is an extension task.

Choose two areas of life covered in this chapter (e.g. education, charity). For each one, research a Mission Statement/Prospectus for a Jewish organization set up in response to Jewish beliefs about that area (e.g. a faith-based school or charitable organization). Write out a key paragraph containing a particular Jewish belief and, underneath it, identify where that belief comes from. You could also compare Jewish responses with those of another faith you have studied.

Glossary

Aleinu Key prayer towards the end of each religious service; describes a better world to come

Anti-Semitism Words or actions directed against Jews

Ark/Aron Hakodesh The focal point of a synagogue; a holy cupboard containing Torah scrolls

Bar/Bat Mitzvah Bar Mitzvah is a Jewish boy's coming of age; Bat Mitzvah is a Jewish girl's coming of age at 12 or 13 years old

BCE Before the Common Era, meaning before Year 1 in the Western calendar

Brit milah Circumcision

Canaan Area described in the Hebrew Bible, roughly corresponding to the land of Israel

Chazan Leader of reading, singing and chanting in the services of some synagogues

Chewing the cud The process by ruminants (mammals like cattle, goats and sheep) of regurgitating plant matter from the first stomach to be chewed again

Chief Rabbi The leader of a country's Jewish community; in the UK, the Chief Rabbi is from the Orthodox United Synagogue

Circumcision The removal of the foreskin of male babies (usually at the age of eight days), by a specially trained Jewish person

Covenant Agreement that God would protect the Jews in return for their worshipping Him and following His commandments

Daven Recite prayers

Egalitarianism Equality; often used in reference to the belief in the equal role of women in Progressive Judaism

Exiled Sent away permanently

Genocide The deliberate extermination of a race or group

Haftarah Passages from Nevi'im (Prophets)

Hagadah A book used at the Seder service, telling the story of the exodus

Halakhah Hebrew for 'the way'; Jewish code of conduct affecting every aspect of living

Hanukkah Eight-day winter festival, in which candles are lit each evening; it commemorates the rededication of the Temple in Jerusalem following the Maccabean victory over the Greeks

Hebrew The language of Jewish sacred texts, written from right to left

Holocaust The Nazi government's systematic extermination of six million Jews during the Second World War; often called the Shoah by Jews (meaning 'catastrophe')

Huppah A wedding canopy, symbolizing the marital home

Israelites One of the Biblical names for the Jewish people

Ivrit Modern Hebrew; the language of the State of Israel

Kasher To purge blood from meat by using salt in order to make it kosher

Kashrut Jewish dietary laws and practices

King Solomon Son of King David and builder of the first Temple in Jerusalem; known for his wisdom, power and wealth

Kittel A white robe worn by men in some synagogues during the High Holy Days; also worn by some bridegrooms and used as a burial shroud

Liberal Judaism The most progressive Movement within Judaism

Lulav Palm wand used as part of the Four Species during Sukkot

Ma'asim tovim Good deeds

Megillot Five Scrolls (Song of Songs, Ruth, Lamentations, Ecclesiastes, Esther); contained in Ketuvim, the third section of the Tenakh

Movements in Judaism Groups in the Jewish community that are different from each other in some beliefs, practices and interpretations (for example, Orthodox, Reform and Liberal)

Oral Torah Words that Orthodox Jews believe were spoken by God to Moses, and then written down much later in the Talmud.

Orthodox Keeping to faith rules and traditions in a strict way

Patriarch The father and ruler of a family or tribe, specifically Abraham, Isaac and Jacob

Persecution Harassment, hurt or putting to death, often for religious or political reasons

Progressive Judaism This term includes all Movements within Judaism which have modernized, adapted or reinterpreted Jewish law (e.g. Masorti, Reform, Liberal)

Promised Land The Land of Israel promised to the Jews by God

Prophets Seers or spokespeople transmitting messages from God

Purim A festival commemorating the rescue of Persian Jews; the story is told in the Book of Esther

Rabbi An ordained Jewish teacher; often the religious leader of a synagogue or Jewish community

Reform Judaism One of the Movements within Progressive Judaism which values the traditions but emphasizes flexibility, individual choice and interpretation in living a Jewish life in modern society

Rosh Hashanah The Hebrew words for 'head of the year'; Jewish New Year celebrated in autumn

Ruach Hakodesh Words or messages inspired by God

Sacrifices Offerings to God of wine and grain, or animals; later replaced by prayer

Secular Without religious reference; non-religious

Seder A festive evening service and meal held in the home at Pesach

Shabbat Day commemorating the creation of the world, when God rested on the seventh day; it begins at sunset every Friday and ends at nightfall on Saturday

Shavuot The Hebrew word for 'weeks'; one of the three pilgrim festivals celebrated seven weeks after Pesach (Passover); it commemorates the giving of the Torah

Shema Central Jewish prayer that affirms the belief in one God, and also promotes living a moral life both at home and in the wider world

Simchat Torah An autumn festival celebrating the completion of the year's cycle of Torah reading (celebrated with much joy and dancing with Torah scrolls)

Split hooves Hooves that divide down the middle, e.g. those of a goat or cow

Sukkot A pilgrim festival celebrated in autumn, when temporary dwellings are built to commemorate the Jews wandering homeless in the wilderness

Synagogue Jewish place of worship; also a place of learning and a community centre

Talmud The first writing down of the Oral Torah (Mishnah), and commentary and interpretation of it (Gemara); a guide to Jewish law

Tikkun olam Repairing the world through carrying out mitzvot; it indicates the belief that humanity shares responsibility with its creator

Torah Judaism's central text; comprises the Five Books of Moses (Genesis, Exodus, Leviticus, Numbers and Deuteronomy), and contains Jewish history and laws

Ushpizin The Aramaic word for 'guests'; the tradition of symbolically inviting spiritual ancestors, like Abraham and Isaac, to the sukkah

Written Torah The Five Books of Moses

Yad A pointer, in the shape of a hand, used when reading the Torah

Yom Kippur The Day of Atonement (eighth day after Rosh Hashanah); a solemn fast day when Jews reflect, pray and repent for their wrongdoing during the year

Index